Turning Toward the Heart

Awakening to the Sufi Way

Turning Toward the Heart

Awakening to the Sufi Way

FORTY QUESTIONS AND ANSWERS

with Shaykh al-Tariqat Hazrat Azad Rasool

FONS VITAE

First published in 2002 by
Fons Vitae
49 Mockingbird Valley Drive
Louisville, KY 40207
http://www.fonsvitae.com

Library of Congress Control Number: 200-211-3222

ISBN 1-887752-46-3

Printed in Canada

بِسْمِ ٱللَّهِ ٱلرَّحْمَٰنِ ٱلرَّحِيمِ

DEDICATION

To all sincere students who are in search of truth.

Contents

The use of the traditional salutation after mention of the Prophet Muhammad in the form of a seal ﷺ has been used throughout the book. It stands for *ṣalla-llāhu ‘alayhi wa āhlihi wa sallam* (may God bless and protect him and his family).

The names of other prophets and of angels are followed by ﵇, which signifies *‘alayhi-s-salām* (peace be upon him).

The names of companions of the Prophet ﷺ are followed by ﵁ or ﵂, which stands for *raḍia llāhu ‘anhu/‘anhā* (may God be pleased with him/her).

The names of Sufi teachers and saints are followed by (r.a.), indicating *raḥmatu-illāhi ‘alayhi/‘alayhā* (the Mercy of Allah be upon him/her).

PREFACE

In today's world, a world fraught with turmoil between nations and individuals and within many hearts, Sufism thankfully opens a doorway of hope. Many people, thirsty travelers in the deserts of modern culture, have been attracted to the luminous water holes where Sufis have congregated and towards which they have guided others. For such desert dwellers, a drop of water, a simple name of God or word of wisdom, is often sufficient. In addition to such travelers, scholars and their students in the universities have become interested in (and some enamored by) songs sung by Sufis such as Rumi, while others have been drawn to study masters of Sufi prose such as al-Ghazālī and Ibn 'Arabī. Hence not only is Sufism significant to many for personal reasons, but the scholarly study of Sufism (also known as Islamic mysticism)—including its literature, philosophy, psychology, and history—has been an important subject within the overall field of Islamic studies in the West for over a century.

Turning Toward the Heart: Awakening to the Sufi Way presents important aspects for the study of Sufism. Written in a concise question-and-answer format, which allows the reader to learn something of the principles and history of Sufism through the lens of a living representative of one of its teaching traditions, the text's central point is not the history of Sufism per se. Rather, this work is one of the mirrors that reflect the human strivings of the spirit within the Sufi tradition for more than twelve hundred years.

Hazrat Azad Rasool represents a line of masters which descends from Sayyid 'Abd al-Bāri Shah, an Indian shaykh of the nineteenth century. In the person of 'Abd al-Bāri Shah six lineages of Sufi masters converged, for he received authorization to teach in the Naqshbandī, Mujaddidī, Qadirī, Chishtī, Shadhilī, and Qaranī Orders. Each of these orders exemplified a formally defined science, unique in its terminology and methodology, part of a spiritual heritage known as *Taṣawwuf*. Most played active roles within the mystical movement that engendered new life in humanity's age-old spiritual quest across the breadth of the Islamic world.

Although for the last eight hundred years Sufism has been characterized by Sufi orders (*tarīqah* (sing.), *turuq* (plural)) under the guidance of Sufi shaykhs, during the formative period (from the eighth to the eleventh centuries C.E.) the orders did not yet exist. Rather, the formative stage of the history of Sufism was characterized by the interplay between the Sufi traditions of Khorasan and Baghdad.* The second major period of Sufism's history was when the Sufi orders were formed, based upon initiatic chains of transmission from master to disciple. One of the most important of these orders was (and continues to be) the Naqshbandī Order, which inherited the tradition of the Khwājagān of Turkestan, the heirs of the Malamatī of Nishapur (in Khorasan), and became the dominant Sufi order in Transoxiana as early as the fourteenth century.

Well-known teachers among the Khwājagān include the founder, Khwājah Abū al-Ḥasan al-Kharqani (d. 1033), and Yūsuf Hamadānī (d. 1140). Whereas some mystics of this era emphasized love for and union with God, the Khwājagān also stressed the overcoming of self. Yūsuf Hamadānī said, "All people know that love is the Supreme Power that unites the human being and God, but no one who is not free from self is capable of love." His successor, Khwājah 'Abd al-Khāliq Ghujduwānī (d. 1179), refined the order's methods of spiritual education, and through his teachings the principles of the order became accessible to a widespread public.

Khwājah Bahā'uddīn Naqshband (d. 1389) was central to the further spread of the order throughout Turkestan. He reformed the practices with an eye toward making them more efficacious. The technique he employed is known as *indirāj an-nihāyah fi'l-bidāyah*—"the embodiment of the end in the beginning"—which in this case refers to his alteration of the sequence in which practices were assigned. Rather than concentrating first on the self, aspirants were directed to concentrate on the heart (*qalb*). Bahā'uddīn Naqshband and his successors believed that being attentive to the heart increased receptivity to the presence of God, and that an influx of divine love could in turn transform the self. Bahā'uddīn Naqshband's central role within the order is evidenced by the fact that from him it took the name by which it is known today.

At the end of the sixteenth century, Shaykh Aḥmad Farūqī Sirhindī (d. 1625) reformed the Naqshbandī order in the domains of both doctrine and practice. He became known as *Mujaddid-i alf-i thānī* ("the Reformer of the second [Islamic] millennium"), and the lineage that descended from him became known as the Naqshbandī-Mujaddidī. Rejecting many of the innovations in Sufi practices that had arisen in India, he affirmed the centrality of Islamic Law (*sharī'ah*) to the spiritual quest. He reaffirmed the Naqshbandī characteristic of involvement in political struggle, as well. He departed from other Indian Sufis in his assertion of the doctrine of the Unity of Being in Vision (*waḥdat ash-shuhūd*), according to which the highest stage of spiritual awakening lies in witnessing or experiencing Union with God while remaining mindful of the distinction between oneself and God. This doctrine repudiated the doctrine of *waḥdat al-wujūd*, or Unity of Divine Being, according to which nothing exists other than God and ultimate union implies identification with God. Also central to Aḥmad Farūqī Sirhindī's reform was a refinement of the Naqshbandī teachings regarding being conversant with the needs of the spiritual aspirants of his time. He identified ten centers of consciousness (*laṭā'if*) within the human body, and he re-organized the practices concerned with these centers. His efforts helped bring about the spread of the order among diverse populations such as the people of Afghanistan, Turkey, and Syria. In the late nineteenth century, additional changes in both the doctrine and practice of the Naqshbandī-Mujaddidī Order were made by Sayyid 'Abd al-Bāri Shah to facilitate students' progress.

The Qadirī Order was founded by Shaykh 'Abd al-Qādir Jilani (d. 1166) of Iraq. 'Abd al-Qādir Jilani was the rector of a school of Hanbalī law and lectured in his *khānqāh* (Sufi lodge) in Baghdad. His sermons, delivered in both institutions, have come down to us today in the work *Divine Discourses* (*al-Fatah ar-rabbani*). As a representative of both the legal and mystical traditions he instituted a system of spiritual training and purification that adhered strictly to the teachings of the Qur'ān and Prophetic Traditions. His sons and other representatives of these teachings spread the rules and doctrines of the order throughout the Islamic world. The order is established today from Morocco to all of Asia Minor and beyond to Malaysia.

Shaykh Abū Is'haq of Syria (d. 940) founded the Chishtī Order, among the most widespread and influential of India. This order played a central role in the Islamization of the multi-religious population of the sub-continent from the tenth century on. It gained an even wider following in the thirteenth century under the leadership of Shaykh

Moinuddīn Chishtī (d. 1236), buried in Ajmer, for whom the order is named today. Among the most pre-eminent personalities of the order was Shaykh Bābā Farīduddīn Ganj-i Shakar (d. 1265-7), whose aphorisms have been assimilated into the Sufi wisdom tradition of India. Shaykh Niẓāmuddīn Awliyā' (d. 1324-5), the most celebrated disciple of Bābā Fariduddīn, led the order through the political upheavals that marked fourteenth-century India, and under his guidance the order extended its influence throughout India. His respect for the holy men of all religions and the belief that service to others is more meritorious than the performance of austerities led him to have a wide following among Muslims and Hindus alike. The mystic call of the order, founded upon the central doctrine of *waḥdat al-wujūd* (Unity of Divine Being), and its commitment to nonviolence, human service, and charitable works determined a social outlook that appealed to a broad spectrum of individuals. Of note is the fact that the Chishtīs did not require conversion to Islam as a condition to instruction in mystic discipline and practices. For the Chishtīs, conversion was a result of the change brought about by the practices of the order, not a pre-requisite to them.

The Shādhilī Order has its roots in the ascetic tradition of North Africa. Shaykh Abū al-Ḥasan Shādhilī (d. 1258), who founded the order in Egypt, was born in Morocco and received his spiritual training there under the instruction of Ibn Mashish (d. 1228). At a time when doctrinal exposition and formal codes of conduct were prevailing and Sufism in Egypt had become a state-sponsored institution, Shaykh Abū al-Ḥasan and his heirs, Abū al-'Abbas Mursi (d. 1287) and Ibn 'Aṭā' Allah (d. 1309), affirmed the synthesizing nature of Islamic spirituality. They stressed the integral relationship of the Qur'anic revelation and correctly guided comportment to gnosis. Students were expected to become well-versed in Islamic law as well as the spiritual disciplines, and were encouraged to maintain a family and professional life. A particularity of the Shadhilī is that it is more a school of spirituality than a centralized institution or Sufi order. From its inception it has retained a flexibility that has allowed its adaptation within multifaceted social and historical contexts. The order is widespread today throughout North Africa and the Middle East in its branches of the Darqāwī, Harraqī, and 'Alawī Orders. In the West, the Shadhilī has found a niche within the interests of many of those seeking a means towards a deeper spiritual life.

Sayyid 'Abd al-Bāri, as an authorized teacher of all the above orders, spent his life transmitting their doctrine and practices. More important, however, than the fact that he represents multiple orders are the changes he brought about in their teachings and transmissions. He applied the Naqshbandī-Mujjaddidī technique of *indirāj an-nihāyah fi'l bidāyah* to the other orders, streamlined the practices, and formulated a "syllabus" or step-by-step progression of spiritual teachings that could be undertaken by aspirants with careers and families. Authorization to teach in the line of Sayyid 'Abd al-Bāri Shah passed to Hazrat Ḥāmid Ḥasan 'Alawī (d. 1959), and from him to Muhammad Sa'īd Khān (d. 1976). The latter's successor is the author of the present volume.

The question and answer format of this work brings to mind the format employed in the earliest works of Sufism, those of Ḥakīm Tirmidhī (d. 869), Ḥārith al-Muḥāsibī (d. 857), and Abū 'Abd al-Raḥman as-Sulamī (d. 1021). It lends the work an air of spiritual companionship, the salient tie that constitutes the teacher/student relationship. The breadth of questions addressed removes the teachings we encounter here from the conceptual or purely academic to the level of lived experience. Azad Rasool does not express himself in complex terms, yet his words convey a depth that draws the reader into the unique nature of the path described. *Turning Toward the Heart* relates, on a variety of levels, to the process of spiritual transformation and a means towards its actualization.

This work is relevant within the domains of human spirituality and psychology for both the specialist and non-specialist. Within the religious studies or history classroom, it offers an example of Sufi methodology from a contemporary teacher of the Islamic spiritual tradition. Those committed to the study of psychology, as the science of the human soul and its states, will find within these teachings an intimate discourse with the self and a wealth of Sufi technical vocabulary developed over centuries across vast geographical regions. Finally, this work offers anyone seeking a deeper understanding of the human spirit a testimony to humanity's timeless spiritual quest.

Kenneth L. Hornerkamp
Athens, Georgia

KENNETH LEE HONERKAMP, a graduate of the Quarawiyyine University of Morocco and the University of Aix-en-Provence, has edited and translated several works of Abū 'Abd ar-Raḥman as-Sulamī (d. 1021), as well as the *Rasā'il al-kubra* of Ibn 'Abbād of Ronda (d. 1390). He presently holds the position of assistant professor in the Department of Religion at the University of Georgia at Athens.

* See introduction to the *Stations of the Righteous* and *The Stumblings of Those Aspiring* by Abū 'Abd al-Raḥman al-Sulamī, K. Honerkamp, Part Two of *Three Early Sufi Texts* (forthcoming Fons Vitae, 2003).

BIOGRAPHY OF THE AUTHOR

Hazrat[1] Azad Rasool was born in the town of Kankroli in Udaipur, India, in 1920. From childhood, he displayed a strong interest in spiritual pursuits. His developing mind quickly became preoccupied with esoteric questions: "Is there some power beyond the physical and mental plane of human experience? Does God exist? If God is One, why do religions differ?" Watching people pray, he wondered: "Are prayers really answered? Or do they just have psychological effects?" Such questions absorbed Hazrat from his earliest years.

Hindus have long held sacred the town of Kankroli, where Hazrat spent his childhood days. A large Hindu temple there attracted pilgrims from all over India, enabling young Azad Rasool to meet many learned and pious people. Even after he had moved away to pursue his education, Hazrat returned to Kankroli during summer vacations. As a young man, he would discuss his questions with the spiritual masters.

Hazrat entered Jamia Millia Institute at the primary level and continued there through his undergraduate studies. Combining his academic efforts and spiritual inclinations, he earned his B.A. in Islamic studies and Arabic. He then went on to receive a second bachelor's degree—this one in education—from Allahabad University.

Two professors at Jamia Millia played significant roles in Hazrat's life. Professor M. Mujeeb, Hazrat's history teacher, had studied at Oxford and authored numerous books, including *Indian Muslims*. Hazrat describes Professor Mujeeb as "a lovely personality," a man who, although not formally a Sufi, possessed the nature and character of a Sufi. Again and again Professor Mujeeb told Hazrat, "Everybody is trying to *take* something. You should become a person who can *give* something." These words deeply impressed the young man, later shaping his choice of career.

A second professor who influenced Hazrat was Dr. E. J. Kallat, a kind and learned Christian. In addition to teaching English, Dr. Kallat supervised the college sports program and served as coach of the hockey team. Hazrat, who was captain of this team, became Dr. Kallat's close acquaintance. "He taught us an important lesson," Hazrat recalls. "He said, 'Make yourself a man. First deserve, then desire.' In other words, you must qualify before you can earn anything." Though not a Muslim, Dr. Kallat enjoined his students to "try to be good, reborn Muslims." He would often invite Hazrat to his home, where they would read and discuss Biblical passages, along with Christian mysticism and other subjects.

Dr. Kallat's respect for different faiths deepened his student's interest in all religions. As Hazrat explains, "I am a Muslim by birth, but I have not always been content with the religion I inherited. The moment I became competent enough to disassociate myself from it, I embarked on the path of investigation with an open mind and heart. I liberated myself from the bonds of traditional authorities and exposed my mind to all influences."

Hazrat explored the validity of many religious systems. He looked for answers to his questions in the sacred texts of different faiths, held discussions with religious scholars and atheists, and became acquainted with modern philosophy and scientific methods. So fond was he of the Bhagavad Gita that he read it over and over again, eventually memorizing parts of it.

Hazrat also studied and experimented with spiritual practices in hopes of determining whether some more permanent reality underlies this phenomenon called "life." He explored yoga and Vedanta, bathing in the sacred waters of the Ganges, living the life of a *bramachari* (a celibate and disciplined student of yoga), and engaging in various other yogic practices. He delved into the academic study of Hinduism, as well. His master's degree in philosophy from Aligarh Muslim University included specialization in both Hindu and Islamic thought.

Yet the yearning within remained unsatisfied. Hazrat had not yet found the path he sought.

After earning his master's degree, Hazrat received an offer to pursue doctoral studies in the United States. He declined. Determined to follow Professor Mujeeb's guidance—to give rather than take—he joined the faculty of Jamia Millia University, although he qualified for higher-paying and more prestigious positions elsewhere. Many of his associates seized opportunities for status and financial gain. But Hazrat remained at the struggling new university, determined to serve its students even at the cost of being ridiculed as "an idealist."

Hazrat's commitment to Jamia Millia reflected his belief that there can be no better work than to teach children and help build their characters. The school's goal was to prepare youths to be good citizens, Indian patriots, and true Muslims, not tools of the "British machinery" that dominated pre-independence India. All the teachers at Jamia Millia worked toward this end with missionary zeal.

At that time, Jamia Millia received no government subsidies. Its revenue came solely from grants, donations, community support, and tuition. Salaries were minimal. Hazrat earned forty rupees a month. Dr. Zakir Husain, Vice Chancellor of Jamia Millia and later president of India, received only eighty rupees. The teachers, however, regarded their work as reward in itself. They performed their duties as worship and strove to work for the sake of work.

Serving children provided one outlet for Hazrat's desire to find meaning in life. He also continued to explore the nature of existence through philosophical and spiritual pursuits. His faculty appointment had made him Professor Mujeeb's associate, and the two met periodically to discuss work. Often they would finish their business in twenty minutes and then spend an hour discussing Sufism in light of contemporary thought and science.

But despite years of seeking and effort, Hazrat remained disappointed. He concluded in his heart that the search he had embarked upon was difficult if not impossible.

Just as Hazrat was nearing despair, his friend R.R. Wahidi told him that the Sufi master Hazrat Shaykh Muhammad Sa'īd Khān (r.a.) was traveling to their area. The shaykh taught Arabic in a school in Azamgharh, U.P., and was coming for a refresher course to Mathura, a town near Vrindravan, not far from Delhi.

Mr. Wahidi suggested that Hazrat meet Shaykh Sa'īd Khān (r.a.). Hazrat agreed. Looking back years later, he said, "I thought, 'All right, I guess I should go. Perhaps I will be able to receive some guidance from this man.'"

Hazrat went to Mathura with a sense of opportunity and hope. Arriving at the mosque, he was directed to the shaykh's quarters. He approached the room, and there he saw a person seated, wearing simple dress and a round cap. The man noticed Hazrat and called him to enter. Hazrat presented him with a letter of introduction, which the shaykh read with approval.

Hazrat then told the shaykh why he had come. He explained that he had been searching for many years and had tested different paths. "If there is something real in your study," he concluded, "please instruct me in it. But if this teaching is only talk to please people, then I would rather not waste your time or mine."

Having heard all this, the shaykh replied, "This path is one of experience. Start, and see what happens." That was all.

This brief statement had an immediate impact. Hazrat has said, "In that moment, I felt detached from the world, and my heart inclined strongly toward the shaykh. I felt love in my heart." Then and there, Hazrat asked Shaykh Muhammad Sa'īd Khān (r.a.) for instruction.

From the time of this initial meeting, Hazrat looked forward to meeting Shaykh Muhammad's shaykh, Ḥazrat Ḥāmid Ḥasan 'Alawī (r.a.). His next winter vacation afforded him the chance. After spending time with Shaykh 'Alawī (r.a.), Hazrat concluded that at last God had granted his prayers. He was fully convinced that he had reached the right person and the right path, the person and path that would quench his thirst and satisfy his inner urge. Thus began Hazrat's journey.

In Sufism, Hazrat found the satisfaction that had so long eluded him. He found deeper meaning also in the religion of his birth. Decades later, he observed, "Now I am a Muslim not because I belong to a Muslim family, but because I discovered Islam through my own yearning, investigation, and experience."

Hazrat studied with Shaykh Muhammad Sa'īd Khān (r.a.) for thirty years, spending time with him while traveling and at his home in Azamgharh. Hazrat tried to be receptive to his shaykh's guidance and instructions; his shaykh responded generously. Eventually, Hazrat received permission to instruct seekers in the sacred and profound teachings of five orders[2] of Sufism: the Naqshbandī, Mujaddidī, Chishtī, Qādirī, and Shādhilī. Finally, a day came when Shaykh Muhammad Sa'id Khan (r.a.) told him, "Whatever I received from my shaykh, I have given to you. Now wait for the blessings of God, for success depends on His mercy and kindness. It does not come from the effort you put forth." He then quoted the Qur'ān: *Allah bestows His blessings upon whom He wills.*[3]

During his early years on the path, Hazrat, like many new students, felt the urge to devote all his time to meditation and prayer. Yet students of *Taṣawwuf*[4] are not asked to renounce the world; rather, they are to be "in the world, not of the world." In the familiar territory of day-to-day life, the seeker's conditioning, biases, and patterns are most deeply set, and it is here that they must be overcome. It is here also that one can serve God and God's creation. When Hazrat told Muhammad Sa'īd Khān (r.a.) that he wished to resign his job and devote himself fully to spiritual practices, the shaykh forbade him from doing so. Performing a worldly job is integral to success on the path, he explained. Hazrat continued to work as a teacher and later became headmaster of Jamia Millia, finally retiring after thirty-six years at the school.

During the lifetime of his shaykh, Hazrat turned his efforts toward making the Sufi teachings more accessible. It had long troubled him that while individuals from all over the world came to India in search of truth, few discovered the benefits offered by the Sufi way. Most inclined toward the better-known schools of Vedanta and yoga. Techniques were easy to come by; gurus circled the globe opening study centers. Signs of real progress, however, were rare, especially of progress that reflected the needs of individuals who had to live and work in contemporary society.

Convinced that Sufism could satisfy the modern seeker's quest, Hazrat conceived the idea of a school offering instruction in the five main Sufi orders. With the consent and guidance of his shaykh, he created the Institute of Search for Truth, located in New Delhi and operating to this day under his personal directorship.

In recent years, Hazrat has established branches of the Institute in the United Kingdom, the United States, Germany, France, Poland, Turkey, and Australia. Years ago, the principle of "living to give rather than to take" led Hazrat to bypass opportunities for travel. Today, this same principle impels him to journey abroad in order to meet students around the world. He works tirelessly to aid seekers in attaining spiritual knowledge, as his own shaykh aided him.

This brief biographical sketch reveals fundamental qualities and requirements of a student of Sufism. The cheerfulness, faith, trust, and sincerity of Ḥazrat Azad Rasool are proven keys to success outwardly and, most importantly, inwardly. His ability to turn each challenge into an opportunity for growth and worship (*'ibādah*) is a sign of the real Sufi.

From his earliest years, Hazrat yearned to discover life's meaning and purpose. He made the effort to seek out a teacher; and, once he had found one, persevered in following the guide's directions until he had attained his goal. All the while, he continued to fulfill worldly roles as husband, father, grandfather, school teacher, headmaster, community leader, and respected elder. Retirement from his profession did not mean retirement from the world. Rather, he dedicated more time to his spiritual mission and service, including the building of the Institute, the construction of a mosque and *khānaqāh* (Sufi study center), and his family duties. In this way, Hazrat Azad Rasool illustrates in practice that which this book describes in words. From his days as a schoolboy to the present, his life has encapsulated what a Sufi is.

This volume addresses both those who know little about Sufism, and those already acquainted with it who desire deeper understanding. The dialogues presented here will introduce novices to Sufism and its benefits. More advanced seekers will find tools to assist in their progress. Both will discover gems of insight and intuition, illuminated by the light of one who has successfully followed the path of *Taṣawwuf.*

In a recent conversation, Hazrat remarked, "I now find myself working and traveling frequently in the West. The task is difficult; but I am hopeful, for God promised Ḥazrat Sayyid 'Abd al Bāri Shah (r.a.), the shaykh of my teacher's shaykh, that this order will spread 'from East to West and from land to sea.' It is in this hope that I am trying my best to do some work in the West. *Inshā'Allāh* (if God wills), one day this effort will be successful."

I have never doubted that in the purity of this man and his teachings lies the formula for peace, well-being, and knowledge of this world (*dunyā*) and the unseen (*ghayb*). For more than two decades, I have been permitted to accompany this saintly guide. Each day, each encounter, whether inner or outer, attests to the verity of the practical, Islamic path of Sufism. Many of my conversations with Hazrat are interspersed with joyful laughter or youthful exuberance. All are filled with insight, wisdom, and a sensitivity that comes only from profound faith, countless hours of meditation, and a reverence for life.

May God continue to sustain the work of my beloved shaykh, Hazrat Azad Rasool, and may God grant him long life, good health, and a presence that embraces many true seekers.

Ahmed Abdur Rashid
Alexandria, Virginia

AHMED ABDUR RASHID (J.E. Rash), founder of the Circle Group and World Community, is the representative of Hazrat Azad Rasool in the United States. An educator, lecturer and writer, he has addressed topics ranging from leadership training and cross-cultural dialogue to peace building, Islam, modernity and applied spirituality through international projects and curricula.

Questions and Answers

OPENING REMARKS

Mysticism is a manifestation of the essence that underlies all religions. Every faith has its inner, spiritual dimension. In Islam, this dimension is known as Sufism or *Taṣawwuf*.

The mystic is graced with an extension of consciousness, leading to a release of latent powers and a widening vision that encompasses aspects of truth outside the grasp of the intellect. He or she has a direct experience of the presence of God—an experience frequently inexpressible in words.

Mystical awareness transcends eras and cultures. Particular mystical traditions, however, rise and fall in popularity according to the needs of time and place. If you lived in Europe four hundred years ago, you probably would not be holding a volume on Sufism. Eastern mysticism had little appeal in Western societies held tightly under the church's sway. But the Enlightenment and the debate between scientific materialism and Christianity ushered in an era of skepticism. Traditional dogma, it seemed, could no longer fully address people's questions and doubts about themselves and their place in the universe.

Toward the end of the nineteenth century, Westerners began looking eastward for answers. The Theosophical Society, established in New York City in 1875, introduced Oriental mysticism to a wider public. In 1883, Swami Vivekananda presented Vedanta at the World Conference of Religions in Chicago. Interest in Vedanta, yoga, and Buddhism grew steadily in the years following.

For many people, interest in Eastern teachings remained superficial. Some, however, began to look for a comprehensive, spiritual approach to daily life. Simultaneously,

Western scholars expanded their activities in Islamic studies. The attention of seekers and scholars alike turned to Sufism.

One of the earliest teachers of Sufism in the West was Ḥazrat Inayat Khan, who pioneered its spread in North America and Europe beginning in 1910. In the decades since, Sufi teachers have established *takīyahs* (learning centers) in the United States, the United Kingdom, and elsewhere outside the Muslim world. Publications on Sufism have also become widely available. In Western metropolitan areas today, one need drive no further than the local bookstore to find Sufi literature, and look no further than the telephone directory to find schools offering lessons in aspects of Sufi practice.

Different *takīyahs* and texts represent varying currents of Sufi teaching. This book is no exception: while addressing Sufism generally, it reflects teachings passed down through the lineage of Ḥazrat Sayyid ʻAbd al-Bāri Shah (r.a.) (d. 1900), an Indian shaykh of the Naqshbandī-Mujaddidī Order who was also authorized in the Chishtī, Qādirī, and Shādhilī Orders. It differs from some of the more popularized presentations of Sufism in several regards.

First, although many Westerners intuit the value of contemplation in seeking a more meaningful life, they often hesitate to undergo the discipline that authentic Sufism entails. Hence certain Sufi circles have taken to viewing *Taṣawwuf* through a superficial, almost occultist filter. In contrast, this book stresses that much effort is needed to attain the fruits of Sufism. It makes clear the importance of performing structured practices under an authorized guide.

A second trend addressed by this book is the desire for generic mystical experiences, which has prompted efforts to divorce Sufism from Islam. Any valid esoteric path is inseparable from the framework of revelation that gave rise to it. Sufism has its roots in the Qur'ānic revelations and in the *sunnah* (example and teachings) of the Prophet Muhammad ﷺ. Yet many would deny its Islamic origin. Muslims who are unfamiliar with Sufi practices and precepts dismiss them as alien to Islam. Non-Muslims who are attracted to esoteric teachings but disinclined toward religion claim that Sufism can be pursued independently. A clearer understanding of Islam among both parties would make evident the inseparability of the Sufi rose from its Islamic rosebush. *Inshā'Allāh* (God willing), the explanations provided in this book may promote such understanding.

Third, the Naqshbandī-Mujaddidī teachings that I share here have received less attention in the West than have the teachings of certain other orders. They differ, for example, from the gnostic trend in Sufism, well-known to academicians. Gnostics hold that unitive experience is the ultimate stage of realization. This perspective was initially articulated by scholarly Sufis of the twelfth and thirteenth centuries, including Abū Ḥāmid al-Ghazālī (r.a.) (d. 1111), who lived and taught in Persia, and the famed Andalucian shaykh, Ibn 'Arabī (r.a.) (d. 1240).[5] The Naqshbandī-Mujaddidī masters expressed the goal of Sufism in another way, focusing on *fanā'* and *baqā'*.[6] They developed a unique approach to spiritual refinement, encapsulated in the saying *indirāj an-nihāyah fi'l-bidāyah*: "where others end, there marks our beginning." These and other features of the Naqshbandī-Mujaddidī teachings are described in the text.

The dialogues presented here originated in conversations with students at the Institute of Search for Truth in New Delhi and at its branches in Europe and the United States, which offer training in the Mujaddidī, Naqshbandī, Qādirī, Chishtī, and Shādhilī Orders. In teaching at these centers, I have found that individuals with an interest in Sufism repeatedly ask certain questions. Their questions provide the framework for the book. I have compiled answers intended to introduce general concepts of Sufism; to explain techniques specific to the Naqshbandī-Mujaddidī Order; and to explore the relevance of Sufism to contemporary Western audiences. I hope that this text will be a guiding and instructive resource for those who genuinely seek the truth.

Today's fast-paced, materially-oriented world challenges us to balance the demands of day-to-day life with the fulfillment of our inner yearnings. Many choices are available in the pursuit of knowledge. Among these choices, it is my experience that the Sufi teachings, transmitted through a chain of authorized teachers, offer a way to lead life in this world within the context of a comprehensive spiritual philosophy. The Naqshbandī-Mujaddidī line of masters in particular has considered the need for practical techniques that can be integrated with work, family, and social responsibilities. Their teachings may benefit readers of different aptitudes and natures today, as they have uplifted seekers for generations.

It is only by the blessings of respected shaykhs of centuries past that the Sufi teachings have endured. I pray that with the blessings of these great masters, God may be pleased with my humble effort to speak plainly about His truth, and that He may accept it.

Azad Rasool
Jamia Nagar, New Delhi, India

The Questions Answered

PART 1: GENERAL TOPICS

Question 1: Sufism

What is Sufism?

The urge toward mysticism—the urge to experience a dimension beyond the material world, to know and return to a spiritual Essence or Truth—is inherent within every person, irrespective of his or her religion. Individuals are imbued with this tendency to differing degrees. Some are endowed with it in quantity; others, only in a small amount. Some people have a chance to develop and translate it into their daily lives, while others do not. Nonetheless, this tendency is present in every human being.

If Sufism is defined as mysticism or the way of the mystic, then its message addresses all people, not just the followers of one religion. Every faith has its own Sufism. In every nation and community there have been Sufis, although they have taken different names and adopted varying practices.

The human being comprises not only a body of flesh, but another aspect, commonly referred to as "I" or "the self" (described in Sufi terms as *nafs*). Mystical experience activates the "I." Like an electrical current, it runs through an individual, bringing forth untapped potentials. With the activation of self comes a certain degree of consciousness and insight. A person starts to sense that his or her "I" reflects another "I"—the "I" of a Supreme Being. He or she becomes conscious of God acting in and through creation.

Many people attain this level of awareness at some point in their lives. An encounter, event, or realization opens them to a reality greater than themselves. For most, this level of awakening is enough. But others desire something more: to contact God, to see the Divine, to experience Truth. Being a mere part is insufficient; they long to annihilate themselves in the Whole, the Eternal. They want their faith to spring forth spontaneously and continuously, like water rushing from a fountain. They yearn to realize in a personal way that *God is as near as your jugular vein.*[7]

How can this yearning be fulfilled? God is the Sublime Being; humans are gross in comparison. Their senses can hear, touch, see, taste, and smell material things, but the Supreme Being eludes detection by these means. How can a particle contact the sun? How can a part become the whole? Human beings from the beginning of time have tried to resolve this dilemma.

According to Sufi teachings, the path to experiencing the Divine Presence starts within. It is said that one who realizes oneself realizes the Lord. God is present, but individuals cannot see the Almighty because curtains of ignorance veil their eyes and rust encases their hearts. The average person is egocentered. Only after he or she has polished the heart and purified the self will the curtains lift, the rust fall away, and the eyes become able to see God.

Through years of effort, Sufi masters developed a scientific approach to achieving such refinement. They discovered that in addition to the mind, human beings have other centers of consciousness that serve as inner faculties for attaining knowledge. Foremost among these centers is the heart. With diligent practice, teachers of Sufism perfected techniques that activate the heart, cultivating profound intuition and realization.

The polished heart becomes a mirror that catches the light of truth and reflects it in one's consciousness. With this light dawns the understanding that beyond material phenomena, there exists a Being of which everything in the universe is a reflection. One's own being itself reflects the higher Being.

Discovering and fulfilling the Divine potential ultimately results in unflinching faith and certainty of truth. One then submits completely to the Almighty, as a drop of rain submits to the ocean. One wills only in accordance with the will of God; all acts are performed for God's sake alone.

Through selfless obedience, the seeker comes to recognize the Presence of the Divine in each event and circumstance. Consciousness of God pervades his or her every moment. He or she becomes a sincere servant of the Almighty. In fact, Sufism is nothing but inward and outward sincerity.

Sufism does not focus only on the purification of the individual. While striving for selflessness, the *sālik* (spiritual traveler) also devotes his or her insights to improving the social and cultural condition of the community, the nation, and humanity as a whole. This commitment to service makes Sufism a dynamic, transformative force on all levels, from personal to global.

Historically, people steeped in the rational intellectual tradition have dismissed Sufism as a speculative pursuit, fueled more by its practitioners' imaginations than by real knowledge. Today, researchers in the fields of human consciousness, quantum physics, biology, chemistry, and psychology are drawing conclusions that parallel premises of Sufism. For example, many scientists now take into account the fundamental interrelatedness of all phenomena. Whether or not they speak in terms of God, their insights echo the mystics' age-old awareness of Divine Unity. Building from points of common understanding, teachers and students of Sufism are engaging scientists in dialogue, working to bridge the gaps between them and thereby help more individuals recognize the benefits of a spiritual view of life.

Like many other disciplines, Sufism has come under the influence of people who lack proper training. Deteriorated forms have emerged. Explaining what Sufism *is* therefore requires attention to what it *is not*. Sufism is not primarily concerned with power or intellectuality. It does not rely on a mixture of cultural techniques and preoccupation with the ego, translated into a quest for greater personal effectiveness, healing abilities, psychic powers, and the like. It is not designed to provide a good living for teachers or heads of organizations, nor does it deliberately keep students in a state of mystification. Westerners—always eager to synthesize themes—may embrace Sufism as a teaching designed to unite all religions and creeds. This, too, misrepresents its focus. Certainly the development of human beings' spiritual potential can diminish intolerance, fanaticism, prejudice, and conflict. But these are secondary results of the Sufi path, not goals.

While diluted derivatives abound, by the grace of the Almighty the essence of Sufism endures. It also remains relevant, offering principles that we can use as bases for our intentions and actions even in the post-modern age. The Sufi path promotes balance between outer life and inner practices—a balance that is becoming all the more important as the pace of life increases.

Other forms of education focus on the mind or the body, on developing skills, professional qualifications, or character. Sufism educates the heart. By developing the heart's infinite capacity to plumb the universe of consciousness, aspirants gain insights that guide their lives and serve as vehicles for understanding self and God. Only the awakened heart can attain God-consciousness; the mind cannot. Those who pursue the Sufi path discover the secrets of awakening the heart. They realize and live the knowledge revealed to the Prophet Muhammad ﷺ by God, Who said, "The earth and the heavens contain Me not, but the heart of My faithful believer containeth Me."

***

Question 2: Comparing Mystical Paths

How does Sufism differ from other unitive and mystical paths such as Buddhism and yoga?

Although I investigated yoga many years ago, Sufism has been my life's study and work, so I can speak with authority only about its teachings. It is not my aim to give detailed comparisons of mystical techniques. My desire is simply to help seekers of truth find their way along the path which I have traveled.

To the extent that Buddhism, yoga, and other spiritual disciplines engender love of humanity, a sense of duty, respect for other people, and yearning for knowledge, they have much in common on an elementary yet significant level. However, they differ from one another and from Sufism both in their methods and in their suitability for particular individuals.

Most paths are associated with the spiritual and cultural heritage of a specific religion. In many cases, this heritage imposes limitations on would-be practitioners. For example, the student of yoga who is not born Hindu cannot be fully integrated into the yogic system, for he or she has no caste or *paratparam* (lineage). The mystical practices of the Jews have a long and distinguished history; but, in keeping with Jewish tradition, they are directed toward individuals who are Jewish by birth. Buddhism advocates monasticism, a lifestyle that suits some people but not others.

By the blessing of God, Sufism has remained a viable tradition to this day. Sufism welcomes people of all religious, cultural, and ethnic backgrounds, just as its container, Islam, calls for protecting the beliefs and practices of members of other faiths. Moreover, Sufism advocates a lifestyle that is in keeping with human beings' natural inclinations.

Sufism also differs from other paths in its approach to personal refinement. Many methods initially stress purification of the self. For example, the practitioner of yoga uses the mind (that is, the conscious aspect of the self) to become attentive. He or she may spend a long time struggling with mental processes and conditioning before becoming open to mystical insights.

In contrast, the Naqshbandī-Mujaddidī *ṭarīqah* (way or path) emphasizes purification of the heart. By using the heart's innate ability to be attentive, seekers enter more quickly into a state of receptivity. Even beginners can learn to turn toward the heart and to direct the heart's attention toward God by means of *niyāh* (intention). Through this practice, known as *murāqabah* (meditation[8]), the student becomes relaxed and responsive to transmission. Only after the heart is transformed does the shaykh guide the student to devote attention to the self and the workings of the mind.

Some mystical paths cultivate extraordinary powers, the development of which may inflate the ego. The Naqshbandī-Mujaddidī way is the antithesis of this. The very act of *murāqabah* encourages humility and patience, through which purification (*tazkīyah*) takes place. The student waits in meditation like the beloved waits for the lover. Sometimes, one waits for years; but the waiting is filled with hope.

***

Question 3: Choosing a Path

How can I know if Sufism is the best path for me?

Teachers in every field rate their own discipline highly. Their testimonials, therefore, are less reliable measures of efficacy than are personal experimentation and intuitive insight. Ultimately, you alone can determine the right way for yourself, weighing how a method applies to your needs and capacity for progress in the context of your personal life.

Several features are important to consider in choosing a path. Given our rapidly changing society, an effective method needs to be adaptable. To cultivate spiritual progress, it must encourage self-discipline. It should take seekers beyond psychological and spiritualistic tendencies, beyond the worshiper or cult mentality. It must help individuals deal effectively with the modern world, and must foster awareness of our interrelationships with and duties toward all living beings.

Based on my own experience, I can say that the transformational Sufism practiced by the Naqshbandī-Mujaddidī Order meets these criteria. Any search for truth is the same to a certain degree, but this order's methods focus on the characteristics described above, and are therefore well-suited to seekers today.

In selecting a spiritual path, novices naturally incline toward the practices associated with their religious upbringing. Many non-Muslims in the West regard Islam as foreign. When they hear that Sufism is the mystical dimension of Islam, they may assume that its techniques are useful only for people from Muslim backgrounds. In reality, individuals may come to Sufism from any background. Whether a person is Christian, Jewish, Hindu, Buddhist, or of another faith by birth, the Sufi practices can help him or her discover new depths of contentment and fulfillment.

***

Question 4: Sufism's Popularity in the West

In recent years, Sufism has attracted growing attention in the West. To what do you attribute this rise in popularity?

Mystical teachings of all kinds have become much sought after in the West, for several reasons. First, Western societies seem to be emerging from an era dominated by rationalism, determinism, and materialism. Where once the intellect reigned supreme, today it is commonly accepted that reason alone cannot arrive at a definitive explanation of reality. More and more people are seeing value in the direct, personal experience of reality that mysticism provides.

The popularity of Sufism also reflects certain widespread concerns and attitudes. People turn to mysticism to alleviate mental and emotional tension, confusion about the meaning of life, fear of death, insecurities regarding the future, and the degeneration of societal values. Some come seeking paranormal phenomena. Others are drawn by the impulse that has motivated mystics of all eras: the yearning for a deeper, more intimate relationship with the Divine.

Sufism responds to these diverse inclinations with a pragmatic approach to balancing inner and outer development. It does not foreclose the highest states of realization to anyone. It not only permits but commends the fulfillment of worldly responsibilities as part of the student's development. While its practices demand time and effort, they are neither so time-consuming nor so strenuous as to be burdensome. The teachings are authentic, developmental, and based on great wisdom. They are loving, and they work.

Sufi training has brought obvious and subtle benefits to countless individuals for hundreds of years. People who encounter students of Sufism are often drawn to the path because they detect in its practitioners something that they themselves like, want, and need. Although they may not fully grasp the magnitude of their need, they nevertheless feel pulled, as if by a magnet.

Sufism, linked as it undeniably is to the Source, has proven that it contains a useful body of knowledge and practice, a route to faith coupled with personal experience. It offers seekers a direct perception of reality, filling a vacuum in cultures that have otherwise lost contact with a viable bridge to the Infinite. I believe this is its most significant appeal; and as human beings East and West continue to seek out the Divine, I anticipate that the Sufi teachings will continue to spread.

***

Question 5: Western Conditioning

What is the difference between Eastern and Western students?

Whether a seeker is Eastern, Western, or both, cultural background cannot be changed, so there is little point in wondering if it makes a difference. The person who undertakes the practices should focus on his or her own performance and refinement, not on comparisons to other students.

Culture in no way determines whether a person qualifies to pursue Sufism. A good Western student is the same as a good Eastern student. Sufism is intercultural. Its methods adjust to the people addressed. Shaykhs of the Naqshbandī-Mujaddidī Order in particular work through transmission, which establishes a personal, heart to heart relationship between the teacher and each student. Whether a person is from East or West, North or South, regardless of race or background, Sufism has the capability of promoting his or her spiritual development.

There are indeed differences between the Eastern and Western mind due to variations in cultural values. These affect how students perceive or react, how they may best be guided or taught, and why they act as they do. The Sufi system of transformation has always been responsive to the time, place, and circumstances. Culture therefore influences how a guide teaches and how the work of the order is carried out.

Yet, at the core, all people are similar in their needs, aspirations, capabilities, and emotional and intellectual sensitivities. Cultural and behavioral differences become irrelevant to a sincere student. This is the beauty of Islam. Its message that all humanity is one community (*ummah*) is a call to overcome prejudice, fear, and bias. Through his or her practices, faith, and submission to God, the Muslim and Sufi transcends destructive and integrates constructive aspects of human differences. He or she values the uniqueness, individuality, and freedom born of variations, while never losing sight of the overriding truth of unity (*tawḥīd*) granted to us by God and taught by the Prophet Muhammad ﷺ.

I am concerned that the conditioning of a Western student might stand in the way of fully benefiting from Sufism. Can a Westerner really achieve the goals you describe?

Yes, of course. Why not? The qualities required to undertake the Sufi path to the Almighty are sincerity, yearning, patience, consistency, and devotion to and love for one's teacher. Easterners do not have a monopoly on these qualities.

If you ask because you are concerned about your own conditioning, let me say first of all that conditioning is inevitable. People everywhere have conditioned responses.

Secondly, conditioning of any kind—psychological, behavioral, or cultural—is relative. It is a learned limitation or viewpoint which prevents individuals from seeing the world as it really is, and from seeing themselves as they really are. Any such limitation is inimical to growth, inimical to the essential freedom of the individual's inner being, and must therefore be transcended.

So, you need to struggle with your conditioning in any case, whether you are interested in Sufism or not! Sufism supports this struggle with techniques that dismantle conditioned viewpoints and erect in their place a true vision of human beings and the universe. Even newcomers to the path frequently find that in doing the preliminary practices, they receive clear proof that they are contacting "something real." This is due to the *barakah* (blessing) and grace that flow from the Origin of revelation itself. With the help of *barakah*, one develops the insight to know that fulfillment is indeed possible. This is one of the most remarkable aspects of Sufism.

***

Question 6: Personal Transformation

You have called Sufism "transformational." Would you elaborate on the changes it brings about, and on how these changes take place?

The Indian master Khwājah Moinuddīn Chishtī (r.a.) (d. 1236) said, "Sufism is neither knowledge nor form, but a particular ethical discipline." A discipline is a way of life, not an armchair study. Sufism is not simply or exclusively about attending lectures, reading books, listening to spiritual music, doing sacred dances, or any combination thereof. It is a dynamic and practical system which requires intense personal effort, for its object is nothing less than the complete transformation of one's character, behavior, attitudes, and conceptualizations.

The student is like a seed planted in the ground. With sun, water, and proper care, the seed grows into a mature plant. Similarly, the interplay between the shaykh and the student, in combination with the *barakāt* (blessings) from God and from the elders, evokes a change within the student's being. At first, as with a seed, change occurs slowly, almost imperceptibly. Gradually, something within the student grows. His or her former being undergoes metamorphosis, until one day, with God's grace, the student has become a completely different being. The Naqshbandī-Mujaddidī Order uses the terms *fanā'* (annihilation) and *baqā'* (subsistence) to describe this process.

The practices are not only transformational, but experiential, for they enable the student to discover for himself or herself the finer details of the principles of the Sufi way. Engaging in this study is like conducting laboratory experiments. You may have been taught that a water molecule contains one oxygen and two hydrogen atoms, but if you synthesize water yourself, your knowledge of its chemistry will be grounded in direct experience. In the same way, a student of Sufism may personally witness what happens along the way. The seeker does not journey in the dark. Although many people consider Sufism mysterious and obscure, it is neither. It is a clear, precise discipline with numerous objective verifications.

Most scientific theories of evolution culminate in the highest primate: the human being. They do not tell us what happens next, within and beyond humans. Several hundred years before Darwin, the Sufi poet Rūmī (r.a.) (d. 1273)[9] stated, "Originally, you were clay. From mineral, you became vegetable. From vegetable, you became animal and from animal, human. During these periods you did not know where you were going, but you were being taken on a long journey nonetheless. You have a hundred different worlds yet to traverse."

Rūmī (r.a.) and other masters tell us that further development awaits human beings. That development depends not on selective adaptation through reproductive succession, as in Darwin's theory, but on consciousness: that is, on a special type of learning that human beings may choose to acquire.[10] Although apparently, the evolution of the physical body culminates in *homo sapiens* ("thinking human"), this is not the end of the story. Additional transformation needs to be undertaken on the spiritual level. Struggle and effort are required to progress toward becoming a whole, perfected person (*al-insān al-kāmil*), the ultimate human goal.

***

Question 7: Humanism and Humanitarianism

Could Sufism be considered a humanistic philosophy? Do students of Sufism undertake humanitarian activities?

Without a doubt, humanism holds high ideals, higher than those of many other ideologies. Historically, humanistic sentiments have elevated all spheres of life, from political and social to religious. Thomas Paine's *Rights of Man* and the French revolutionaries' cry of "liberty, equality, fraternity" are but two examples.

Sufism differs with the humanists' secular premises but shares their humanitarian aims. Those who travel the Sufi path make love of God their aim in life, and it is said that the way to the love of the Lord passes through the valley of service. Many Sufi masters (including some of the great Chishtī shaykhs of India centuries ago) have adopted service as a means to attain the love of the Almighty. God rewards humanitarian efforts by blessing the aspirant with further spiritual development—a transformation that humanist and mystic alike recognize to be the perfection of our humanity.

However, humanitarian acts should be viewed as means to an end, not ends in themselves. It is misleading to consider them otherwise. I am reminded of two quotations that underscore the relationship between serving God and serving humans. A famous Indian poet once said, "So many slaves of God wander as ascetics in the forest. I see no value in their way; I prefer to be enslaved to one who loves one's fellow creatures." An eminent Indian politician observed, "God, I can deny; man, I cannot."

Humanism is a noble ideal. But if the pursuit of the dignity of human beings supplants the pursuit and worship of the transcendent Reality, then we are following a track that is misguided if not dangerous. Our primary goal should be to strive toward the Divine Reality.

Some might say it is selfish to focus primarily on inner, personal refinement. But the opposite argument can also hold true: serviceful acts may end up serving one's own ego or interests more than others' needs if one has not attained selflessness.

Individuals' outward lives always reflect their internal conditions. The injustices and inequities addressed by humanitarians originate in qualities of the unrefined self: greed, envy, hatred, egotism. By improving individuals inwardly, Sufism influences their actions. By influencing actions, Sufism permeates and benefits society.

***

Question 8: Global Issues

Does Sufism address global issues such as environmental degradation, poverty, and conflict?

The Sufi approach is relevant both to today's society and to questions that will shape humanity's direction in the future. Issues relating to community values, cultural diversity, environmental preservation, economic equity, and conflict resolution are all considered in the teachings of Islam. Historically, various Sufi masters sought to address these issues. Today, those engaged in Sufi practices are applying ttheir knowledge of *Taṣawwuf* to fields as varied as sustainable development, education, therapy, parenting, science and technology, and cross-cultural communication.

But Sufism's greatest tool for addressing global issues is not its tradition of social action. As I have said, disciples of Sufism view service as a means, not an end. Outer work alone cannot resolve the problems that beset humanity, for these problems' roots lie in the human heart. Attempts to deal with problems on the level of the problems may succeed; more likely, they will not. We must look beyond external manifestations into the hearts of human beings everywhere—and, more specifically, into our own hearts. If a person's heart is noble, if his or her feelings are refined and enlightened, then that person will not burden the world. That person will not be part of the problem, but part of the solution. If more people consciously undertook to enlighten their own hearts, then they would each become part of the answer to global needs. If conferences, committees, and councils were staffed by Sufis, the world would not be in the state it is in!

Dedicated practice of Sufism makes for an increasingly integrated and transformed human being. Such a person can only benefit his or her community and society as a whole. There is, I am sorry to say, a pressing need for such people—for people who, while fulfilling their outer responsibilities, are also inwardly attentive and refined. Our societies need people who act from their hearts, with hearts that are refined and loving.

No one can change the world single-handedly. Each person can change himself or herself and, having done so, influence others to do the same. Sufism is not now, nor has it ever been, a mass movement. It operates on an individual level. It attempts to light candles in the darkness. In this way, Sufism yields a particular harvest within society. Today, more than ever before, society needs the fruits of that harvest.

***

Question 9: Stress, Angst, and Depression

What effect might Sufi methods have on conditions such as stress, angst, depression, and neuroses?

It is always tempting to suggest that a single system can cure all problems. Experience suggests otherwise. Essentially, a candidate for training in the Naqshbandī-Mujaddidī Order should be balanced both psychologically and emotionally; otherwise, he or she may encounter difficulties on the path.

Certainly, the hours devoted to the practices will help with what you call stress. *Murāqabah* (meditation) improves the health of the body's physiology and nervous system. Sufi training is particularly relevant for individuals who suffer from angst, which often stems from a lack of purpose and meaning in life. As for depression, in many cases this condition responds favorably to challenge. The greatest challenge an individual can undertake is self-transformation.

Beginning students often comment on the peace of mind that develops through the practices, sometimes quite quickly. Sufi teachers do not consider this a goal in and of itself, but it can be a positive byproduct of engaging in spiritual work.

***

Question 10: Psychotherapy

Many people today are focused on the importance of psychological well-being. How do Sufis regard psychology? Could Sufism be viewed as a religious form of psychotherapy?

The answer to your question requires some historical context. Ancient and pre-industrial cultures valued non-ordinary states of consciousness as venues for learning about hidden aspects of existence. Traditionally, visionary states were viewed as important sources of knowledge not only by the mystics of Islam, but also by the mystics of Christianity, Hinduism, various indigenous communities, and other societies. The scientific and industrial revolutions changed this view. Reason and intellect replaced spirituality and faith as the measures of all things. For many, mystical experience no longer qualified as a legitimate route to understanding.

In the late nineteenth century, the field of psychiatry emerged. Non-ordinary states of consciousness came to be seen as "diseases." Some early psychiatrists drew no distinction between psychosis and mysticism: both were abnormalities, warranting medication.

Later psychiatrists, notably C.G. Jung, began to re-evaluate the relationship between psychological and spiritual well-being. Some states that psychiatry had dubbed "mental aberrations" were recognized as natural self-healing processes of the psyche and body.

Beginning in the 1960s, interest in spiritual experiences and consciousness grew in the West. Many individuals became deeply involved in mystical practices, especially meditation. Step by step, spirituality started to make a comeback. Transpersonal psychology and other approaches forged bridges between the scientific and spiritual traditions. Today, more and more people are acknowledging the price that society has paid for neglecting modes of faith and experience that nourish, empower, and give meaning to life.

Those who strive in the way of *Taṣawwuf* respect contributions to human knowledge made by the fields of psychiatry and psychology. However, Sufism embraces a clear understanding of mind and consciousness, and it has possessed this knowledge far longer than contemporary psychology. Furthermore, the Sufi understanding of psychological, emotional, and behavioral processes has always been practical and integrative. Secular psychotherapy aims to re-establish inner harmony and to enable individuals to function healthily within the family and society at large. Sufism not only re-integrates an individual's psychic components, but links the person with his or her Creator. In no way can Sufism be considered merely a religious form of psychotherapy. Such a notion misrepresents the intimate and awesome mystery experienced in the Sufi aspirant's heart: the direct communication opened between God and human being.

What do you think about psychological training seminars, encounter groups, and the like? Can these promote spiritual transformation?

I cannot speak with direct experience of these techniques. Over the years, some students have reported to me their experiences with them. Based on that information and on my own feelings, I believe that such techniques might assist some people, but their usefulness for spiritual seekers is limited.

Certainly, the types of seminars and groups that you mention can have constructive effects. My concern is that their effects may be short-lived, for their training usually does not alter the participants' deep-seated cultural and psychological conditioning. Therefore, rather than viewing these programs as methods for transformation, we might better describe them as means for ego rearrangement, frequently focused on overcoming personality issues, difficulties in relationships, or problems of self-esteem. Being culturally based (for the most part), they do not reach beyond their inherent limitations to address human beings' spiritual potential or the global issues we confront today. I have to say that they are not where students of Sufism should place their interest.

***

Question 11: Gurdjieff's Teachings

Can seekers attain perfection through Gurdjieff's teachings?

I am not a Gurdjieffian, so I cannot answer from the point of view of one who has sought perfection in this way. I do know that Gurdjieff traveled throughout the East and gained a certain amount of insight. However, it is obvious to teachers in the East, especially in the Naqshbandī Order,[11] that Gurdjieff did not complete his work. I am sure that what he had to offer benefited his companions and students at the time, but since his work was incomplete, it was not properly and fully understood.

Students can progress only as far as their teachers can take them. The person who studies Gurdjieff's methods alone may go as far as Gurdjieff went—but no further. If you wish to travel to a mountain pass in the Himalayas, you can fly to Dehra Dhun, and from there, take a bus a little further into the mountains. Where the bus stops, you can catch a horse cart. Eventually, you will reach a point beyond which a cart cannot proceed, and you must walk the rest of the way. The vehicle provided by Gurdjieff takes people only so far. From what I gather and from what I have seen personally, it does not allow students to complete the journey.

I know of a number of individuals who have studied the teachings of Gurdjieff, then sought out representatives of the Naqshbandī Order in hopes of finding the source of his work. People would not seek the source if they were satisfied with what they already had. We are grateful for all vehicles that bring students to our door, and we respect their methods and practitioners. Nevertheless, we also recognize that approaches suited to one place and time may not be appropriate to others. It seems that Gurdjieff's methods lack relevancy today, and for this reason, contemporary Naqshbandī teachers generally do not use them.

***

Question 12: Women's Roles

There is much discussion these days about women's roles in society. Would you please comment on this subject in terms of Sufism and Islam?

The Qur'ān states that men and women were created equally, from a single soul, to complement one another.[12] Islam and Sufism contain no statement that God created woman out of the rib of Adam عليه السلام as a creature of lesser worth, a subordinate or appendage to man.

True Islam promotes the social, political, and economic equality of the sexes. It establishes the same ethical obligations, rewards, and punishments for men and women. All Muslims, regardless of gender, are enjoined to seek knowledge. Lectures by the Prophet Muhammad ﷺ were attended by women and men, and since that time, women have numbered among the respected scholars of Islam. Muslim women as well as men are entitled to own, sell, manage, and make contracts governing property. If a woman commits a crime, her penalty is the same as a man's. If she is wronged or harmed, the compensation due her is likewise the same.

These and other rights established by Islam in the seventh century significantly advanced women's status. Critics have claimed that Islam denigrates women. This is not the case. The lesser treatment accorded women in some Muslim societies reflects deep-rooted cultural traditions and prejudice, not the teachings of the Qur'ān or *sunnah* (example and guidance of the Prophet Muhammad ﷺ).

As for Sufism, all students are treated according to their sincerity, capacity, and yearning. Creed, color, culture, and gender are irrelevant. Women and men can achieve equally high stations, as is evident in the number of female saints (*awliyā'*[13]) throughout history. In fact, women who are genuinely sincere sometimes progress faster than members of the opposite sex. Because they are by nature more sensitive, their centers of consciousness may be awakened more quickly than those of men.

***

Question 13: Factors for Success on the Journey

Which factors or qualities are most essential to success in the Sufi way?

There are four major considerations for a person who adopts this path: motivation, support from the teacher, singleness of purpose, and dedication.

Motivation or intention is the most important element in everything a person does. The Prophet Muhammad ﷺ said, "Actions are [judged] by intention." For instance, take this woolen shawl which I have wrapped around myself. It could reflect a variety of intentions. One is to ward off the cold. A second is to attract the attention and respect of others, to make me feel different or important. The act of wearing the shawl is the same, but my intention alters its significance.

Consider another example. A man went to a mosque, sat in a corner, and started doing recitations evoking remembrance of God (*dhikr*) with the intention that people should notice him and consider him pious. Those who saw him said, "This fellow is trying to hoodwink us." Every day, he sat doing *dhikr*; every day, people called him a fake. Finally, he thought, "Day after day, month after month, I've wasted my time making a show of doing recitations. Perhaps I should try to really do *dhikr*. It might accomplish something." After he altered his intention, people began to say, "It wouldn't hurt to be nice to this fellow. He's not a bad man. In fact, he's good and pious." They changed their attitude.

The seeker should contemplate his or her purpose in undertaking the path. I say to each of my students, "Please ask yourself: 'What do I want from doing all this?'" People do not respond clearly, but I am of the opinion that 75%

have a different intention than what they state. The sole motivation of a seeker of truth should be the search for truth, nothing else.

Very few students follow this guidance. Most hope to find some magical shortcut to their objectives. Students whose aim is other than the search for God sooner or later give up.

The second consideration is the support of the shaykh. The aspirant finds a teacher and then establishes a formal relationship with him or her. However, the formal relationship is less important than the relationship between hearts, known as *rābiṭah*. *Rābiṭah* refers to a connection based on affection, love, and trust—on inner attraction and reflection, not outer desires and recognition. It should be informal in expression, not formal.

Sometimes the teacher, drawing from the resources of his or her own being, lifts the student's state to assist in his or her spiritual travel. Imagine that you are walking with a child, and you come to a brook too wide for the child to jump over. What do you do? You pick up the child, then cross the brook. Similarly, the teacher lifts the student spiritually over obstacles, from one stage to another. These obstacles might be likened to locked doors. The student progresses some distance, then confronts a door that is firmly sealed. The doorkeeper says, "You cannot go beyond this point. You will never open this door unless you apply more effort and perseverance." But the teacher comes to help, declaring that such a true seeker does not need more practice. He or she takes hold of the student's hand and escorts the student over the threshold.

Unless a relationship of love and affection is established between the teacher and the student, such difficulties cannot be resolved. The help of the teacher will not be available.

I give these examples to clarify the difference between a formal relationship and an informal, heart-to-heart, spiritual relationship. The physical presence of the teacher is not necessary. The teacher may be miles away, but if a bond exists between hearts, his or her presence will be felt and be effective. There is a Sufi saying: "Heart works with heart." Heart is connected to heart, and when the shaykh and student meet, it is a meeting of hearts.

In sum, the seeker needs the spiritual support of the teacher, and this support is available through *rābiṭah.*

The third consideration is singleness of purpose. After the student achieves the first two goals—a clear intention and the support of the teacher—the third is to give up all other pursuits and focus on one purpose. A student should not continue looking here and there in search of something new. Given the human tendency to like some aspects of one place or method and other aspects of another place or method, one could spend one's whole life going from door to door, never settling down long enough to realize the full benefits of any discipline. Trying to pursue multiple paths simultaneously is like trying to sail in two boats at the same time.

The student should proceed single-mindedly in one direction, concentrating on the sole object to be achieved. Sometimes it is said that Sufism means looking in only one direction and seeing all things as one.

Have you ever climbed a mountain? You catch a glimpse of the peak and are inspired to reach it. But you cannot get there in a single leap; you must ascend step-by-step. During every moment of your climb, you are absorbed by the step you are taking. You are not worrying about what will happen tomorrow. You focus on following your guide, lest you stumble from the path. You are intent upon keeping your equipment in good working order; you cannot afford to lose your pick or let your rope fray. Sometimes, you face snow squalls or other difficulties. At other times, you are able to rest along the way. As you climb, you occasionally find yourself walking downhill, crossing valleys and plains. But at all times, you maintain your singleness of purpose. Even when clouds cover the peak, you know you once had clear sight of it, and you draw inspiration from that vision. Finally, you achieve your goal. You reach the top, gaze out across a magnificent vista, and forget all the difficulties of the journey. This is the outcome of singleness of purpose.

Whenever my students write to me, I write in reply, "May God grant you dedication, perseverance, and consistency." These qualities are the fourth consideration that I mentioned. Their core lies in remaining firm in one's efforts. In undertaking this path, you are committing yourself to be punctual and regular in all the practices. It should not happen that one day you do your prayer and meditations, but the next day you have guests or a heavy workload, so you choose not to do them. Steadiness and firmness mean that whatever the hour of night or day, you will not fail to complete, on time, that which has been assigned. If this type of consistency is observed, your travel on the path will be much easier.

***

Question 14: Difficulties on the Spiritual Path

I have heard that the Sufi path can be quite challenging, and that simply persevering in these studies is an accomplishment. Is the path itself difficult, or do the difficulties attributed to it stem from some other source?

You raise a good question. If we are talking about challenges, we should keep in mind that in the past, aspirants performed all kinds of arduous practices. They would engage in *dhikr* (remembrance of God) by holding the breath for a long time. They would fast until they were in agony from hunger. During forty-day spiritual retreats, they would undertake exercises such as hanging head-down in a well while doing recitations. In eras when Sufism demanded this degree of discipline, perseverance was indeed a great accomplishment.

In most Sufi orders today, strenuous practices are no longer the norm. The Naqshbandī-Mujaddidī Order, for example, only requires students to sit patiently in *murāqabah* (meditation) and wait to receive the blessings and favors of the Divine. Perseverance in this case does not mean withstanding onerous trials, but simply devoting the time required. Let us say there are two students, one doing the practices diligently, and the other, less so. Perhaps the first devotes four hours a day to meditation, while the second sits for only three. Assuming that both students are sincere in their efforts, the one who sits longer will receive the greater benefits.

Unlike other disciplines, the Naqshbandī-Mujaddidī practices which I teach require no particular posture, nor must one do lengthy recitations. A student may sit for an hour in *murāqabah*, but emerge feeling as if only five minutes had passed. He or she sits and loses awareness of self, as though drifting. *Murāqabah* is like knocking at a door, ringing the bell, and then settling down in a comfortable place to wait for the door to be opened. I cannot understand why such practices would be considered difficult.

As you have suggested, difficulties arise from a different source: psychological and social conditioning. Certain syndromes that abound in the modern world—excessive sensitivity, imagining oneself to be perfect, being convinced one is psychologically ill—are especially likely to generate difficulties. The path is not designed to cause pain and suffering or make life miserable. On the contrary, it leads to happiness and fulfillment. The process of refinement, however, involves facing one's own weaknesses and faults, which can be quite challenging at times.

The crux of the issue lies in what motivates a seeker more: the urge to achieve nearness to the Divine, or the desire for security and ease. Let me return to the analogy of mountain climbing. A person wants to scale Mount Everest. He or she knows the trek will entail many hardships; it may even be life-threatening. But that individual is so determined that he or she sacrifices everything—health, wealth, employment, status—to attain the goal. Paying no attention to difficulties, such a person eventually reaches the peak.

Here is another well-known example. A famous king fell in love. He could not remain king and marry the woman he loved, so he abdicated the throne. He sacrificed the crown for the sake of his love.

Difficulties may be overwhelming, or they may be overcome, depending on one's motivation. How urgently do you desire to come nearer to God? Are you willing to do what is necessary to fulfill that desire? If your motivation is correct, then all psychological and social difficulties will pass. You will make sacrifices[14] willingly because of your yearning to achieve the love of God.

There is an Urdu couplet: "The sea is on fire and one must cross the sea." Difficulties always exist. To persevere on the spiritual journey, one's desire to reach the other side must be powerful enough to subdue any fire.

***

Question 15: Love and Transformation

Many Sufi books mention love as a technique of transformation. To what degree do you use this method?

Love is a powerful technique used extensively by Sufi shaykhs for re-awakening their students. Historically, some teachers laid such importance on love that when students applied for training, they were asked if they had ever been in love. If an applicant answered no, he or she was told to go away, fall in love, and only then come back to study. The faculty of love helps bring human beings close to God, for the more one loves God, the nearer one draws to Him.

Sufi masters use love as a tool for developing sensitivity to the Creator. To become attuned to God, a student must first achieve unity between his or her outward being and inward being. Without unity of inner and outer, one's character remains fragmented. Disharmony between the aspects of one's life leads to anxiety and depression, and these states interfere with turning toward the Divine.

Love of the shaykh is one means through which students may attain psycho-physical harmony, becoming liberated from mental states that block spiritual progress. The student's self-identity is linked to that of the teacher through the attractive force of the teacher's sincerity and love. Based on the connection to the teacher (whose character is already unified), the seeker also establishes unity of character.

Traditionally, Sufi guides have spoken of *fanā' fī' sh-shaykh*—literally, "annihilation in the shaykh"—a stage in which lower attributes are eliminated as love for the shaykh subsumes the ego. Such overpowering affection for the teacher is meant only to be a transitional step between self-absorption and absorption in God. Next the teacher guides the student to focus on the Prophet Muhammad ﷺ, an individual who, by virtue of being both fully human and a recipient of Divine guidance, attained a level of perfection that may serve as a model for the seeker's own life. As love for the Prophet ﷺ grows, the student progresses toward "annihilation in the Prophet ﷺ," or *fanā' fī'r-rasūl*, coming into harmony with the qualities demonstrated through his life and guidance (*sunnah*). The shaykh then directs the student's focus toward God. The student becomes increasingly absorbed in remembrance of God until he or she transcends the limitations of the ego and its associations. At length the stage of *fanā' fī'llāh* ("annihililation in God") may be reached. Separation from God, the Beloved, the Source of love itself, dissolves as the student becomes a perfect servant of the Divine.

These techniques, based on love, were commonly employed by the early Sufi masters and are still widely used. But they entail certain risks, for it is not easy to differentiate between spiritual love and temporal love. How is a student to attain the pure and sincere love that leads to spiritual unification with the teacher? It cannot be achieved merely by talking about love; rather, it evolves as one spends time with the shaykh and applies oneself to the study. Unfortunately, love today has broader connotations than in previous centuries. It has come to imply a strong emotional response, often accompanied by sexual attraction, lack of permanent commitment, and promiscuity. In a culture that has firm values and virtues, where love has a clear meaning apart from these connotations, and where there is loyalty, trust, and a deep commitment to family, love may still be a suitable technique. But in a society where the culture has degenerated, this technique elicits feelings and intentions that may endanger rather than assist a seeker's progress.

We hear much about love in the stories of *awliyā'* (saints) such as Rabi'ah (r.a.) (d. 752 or 801), Junayd (r.a.) (d. 910), and Shiblī (r.a.) (d. 946).[15] The love experienced by these masters is not to be confused with infatuation based on physical attraction or with "falling in love" as we know it today. When one has transformed the lower self (*an-nafs an-ammārah*), the beauty one perceives and the love one feels is comprehensive, energizing, and spiritually fulfilling.

Today, shaykhs of the Naqshbandī-Mujaddidī Order continue to guide students toward experiencing pure, all-embracing love; but they do not do so by using love as a technique of transformation. Instead, they emphasize transmission (*tawajjuh*), the affinity or congenial relationship between the teacher and student (*nisbah)*, meditation *(murāqabah),* and the concept known as *indiraj an-nihayah fi'l-bidayah* ("where others end, there marks our beginning"),[16] for they have found these approaches to be the most effective, safe, and appropriate for modern-day societies.

***

Question 16: Progress

How would you define progress in the context of the Sufi path?

Sufism is a journey. A person who drives from Delhi to Paris gains detailed understanding of the route and landmarks along the way. Similarly, while traveling on the spiritual path, a student gradually develops intuition about himself or herself, about others, and about life in general, and thereby comes to see the signposts of progress. I can describe some of these signposts; others become clear only when one discovers them for oneself.

Having read about visions and miracles in stories of Sufis of the past,[17] many students assume that as they progress, they also will experience out-of-the-ordinary phenomena. Among my own students, I have found that those who see or have *kashf* (visions or intuitive insight[18]) feel satisfied that they are making progress, while those without *kashf* worry that they are getting nowhere.

Visions and phenomena may be pleasing, but the reality of improvement is far, far removed from such experiences. The practitioners of certain paths may content themselves with receiving "guidance" from visions revealed by the imagination. They may believe they have achieved enlightenment, even when they have not progressed beyond the first stage of the self, *an-nafs al-ammārah.*[19]

In fact, among students on the spiritual journey, those who have *kashf*—and those who do not—hold the same position. The person who sits in meditation makes progress, with or without phenomena. Let's say you and another person are passengers in the same car. If you are sitting in the front seat, you can see both the driver and the scenery. The other person, seated in back, may not see either very well. But when the car reaches the destination, both of you arrive there.

Whenever you sit in meditation, you receive *barakāt* (blessings). It is one thing to receive blessings, and another to be aware of receiving them. Receiving is the main object. Even if you do not feel or see anything, even if you do not have detailed knowledge about what you are receiving, do not be disappointed. You still will reach the destination.

The phenomena associated with earlier mystics had some connection with their way of life. An individual who rarely interacts with other people and who takes little food—only grain and water, for instance—will be highly receptive to *kashf* (visions) and other mystical experiences. But today, few seekers can adopt this lifestyle.

Sometimes students who do not perceive visions or phenomena advance more rapidly than those who do. They are humble because they are not "seeing" anything. Extraordinary experiences may become sources of gratification linked to this world (*dunyā*), rather than means of attracting the seeker to the unseen (*ghayb*), since they usually pertain more to creation than to the Creator. As the Indian scholar and mystic Shaykh Aḥmad Farūqī Sirhindī (r.a.) (d. 1624) explained:

> The object of the Sufi *sulūk* (journey) is not to view forms and images of transcendental realities, or [to] behold colors and lights. In fact, [these] are nothing more than play and fun.... Forms, these or others, and lights, physical or spiritual, are all created by God. He transcends them all, and they are nothing but His signs and proofs.[20]

The true student is interested in God alone and finds phenomena to be other than God. Rejecting them, he or she focuses on the Creator, not on the created.

What are the criteria of progress, if visions and phenomena are not? A simple way of judging one's forward movement is to watch for improvements in behavior and conduct. As an individual performs the practices, his or her character and personality gradually change. Certain weaknesses or other problems (for example, addictions and similar tendencies), slowly subside. With the purification of the heart, evil tendencies of conceit, greed, and jealousy also recede.

Another criterion is best explained by means of an analogy. Often when a person becomes deeply involved in his or her work, he or she forgets to eat, rest, and so forth. Analogously, many people become so much involved in worldly affairs that they forget to remember God. Those who pursue the way of the Sufi strive instead to become so engrossed in remembrance of God that none of their worldly activities distract them from this recollection. Everything in life may serve to remind them of the Presence of the One Who created it.

Let's say that a woman learns from her physician that she has contracted a terminal illness. For months or even years afterwards, she continues to eat, sleep, and share the company of her family and friends, just like other people. Yet for her, the beauties and bounties of day-to-day life take on new significance. The sweetness of time spent with her children reminds her that such times are finite. Her husband's companionship heightens her awareness that soon they may be parted. The realization that nothing is permanent suffuses every aspect of her life, causing her to appreciate all she has been given. Similarly, while a disciple of Sufism carries on working, eating, engaging with family, and performing other daily activities, he or she is constantly aware of God. This awareness inspires him or her to strive to be a better person, to show compassion, withhold anger, avoid greed and self-centeredness, repent for errors, overcome character flaws, seek God's forgiveness: in sum, to approach all worldly relationships and activities within the context of the single paramount relationship between oneself and the Divine.

Two seekers were on their way to see a famous shaykh when they passed some cats in conversation. To their surprise, they could understand the cats' words. One cat remarked that the shaykh whom these men sought had died. Greatly saddened by this news, the two were unsure whether to proceed. One man said, "Let's return home." But the other said, "We've come all this way. Let's continue our journey, visit the tomb of the shaykh, and offer prayers for him there." And so they traveled on.

At length they arrived in the shaykh's town and asked where he was buried. The villagers replied, "We can't direct you to the tomb, because the shaykh is still alive!"

Puzzled, the travelers sought out the shaykh and told him of their experiences. He asked, "When exactly did you hear that I was dead?" They recalled the day and time. He explained, "At that particular moment, I had forgotten God; so, in the higher realms, it was announced that I had died."

The student can distinguish by degrees how much he or she has turned from worldly affairs to Divine affairs. Beginners on the path remember God periodically, through assigned practices such as *wuqūf al-qalb* (heart pause) and *murāqabah* (meditation). The rest of the time is passed remembering things other than God. Gradually, students start to sustain their remembrance of God for longer periods and are less frequently distracted by material concerns. Finally, consciousness of God permeates every moment of their lives. This unceasing remembrance is the goal of one who travels the Sufi path, and the signs of its gradual attainment are the best proof of progress.

***

Question 17: Sufi Lifestyles

Is it required that people on the Sufi path adopt a particular lifestyle? For example, must they give up material possessions, practice self-denial, or detach themselves from worldly affairs?

To varying degrees, Sufi aspirants and masters in centuries past considered renunciation, austerities, self-denial, and even (in some cases) mortification of the body necessary for success on the path. Such endeavors suited the circumstances and temperaments of these saintly individuals, enabling them to attain great heights of spiritual refinement, thereby making their lives examples of what the human soul can achieve. We, however, live in a very different era.

Today we are pressured from all sides. Numerous demands weigh upon us: we must earn a living, look after our families, take active roles in our communities. We all have fundamental needs for livelihood, security, shelter, food, and the other requirements of life. But as society has become more complex, our definition of "needs" has widened. Today's necessities include cars, computers, e-mail accounts, insurance—and the list goes on. All too often, we mistake wants for needs, to our own detriment.

Given this tendency, we certainly could learn from the lives of our predecessors. For example, as a young man growing up in India, Ḥazrat Nizamuddīn Awliyā' (r.a.) (d. 1325) was a top academic student and an expert in debate. But he felt so strongly drawn toward the spiritual life that he renounced everything and went to live with his shaykh, Bābā Farīduddīn Ganj-i Shakar (r.a.) (d. 1265) in Ajodhan (present-day Pak Pattan, Pakistan). Once an acquaintance from school came to visit and saw him dressed in simple, tattered clothing. This friend said (quite frankly, because they had been classmates), "You were an excellent student. You could have been a successful man, earning lots of money. I don't understand why you chose this life!"

Bābā Farīd (r.a.) knew from his spiritual insight what was happening outside his chamber. After the man left, he called Ḥazrat Nizamuddīn (r.a.) to him and asked, "What did your visitor say?"

Ḥazrat Nizamuddīn (r.a.) replied, "He said that I could have been successful and had a good job, in which case I wouldn't have to wear this kind of clothing."

Bābā Farīd (r.a.) remained silent. But he used his spiritual powers, and suddenly a tray of sumptuous dishes appeared before them. He handed the tray to Ḥazrat Nizamuddīn (r.a.), instructing him to take it to his friend.

The shaykh demonstrated that Ḥazrat Nizamuddīn (r.a.) was not at a loss. Even in poverty, if the students of his *ṭarīqah* (order) desired material provision, they had the power to obtain it. They were simply detached from the world, and therefore not interested in possessions.

A second example is this. A mendicant used to meet regularly with a particular Sufi master. They became good friends, to the point that one day, the mendicant said, "As you know, I take great pleasure in your company. I have never revealed this to anyone before, but I know the secret of making gold. Because you are such a fine person, I think I want to tell you my secret."

The Sufi kept quiet, but his friend insisted. Finally, the Sufi looked around the room, and everything his gaze touched turned to gold instantly.

The Sufi did not desire wealth, though had he wished, he could easily have had it. The mendicant, on the other hand, had worked long and hard to gain the power to create riches, and he was certain he had a great secret to share.

Perhaps you have heard or read similar stories before. Such stories are not told to entertain or to impress people with mystical powers. They serve another purpose: to convey a message about the relationship between human beings and the material world.

One mystic wrote, "If it be the Sufi's station, he [or she] will be found herding the sheep one day, sipping from a golden goblet with a king the next." Many non-Sufis have formed a narrower picture of how disciples of Sufism live and act, associating them with seclusion, exotic costumes, self-imposed poverty, austerities, chanting, whirling, or other practices. Different orders may be characterized by none, some, or many of these features. But in all cases, such practices are only forms. Forms serve a purpose in the training of the student, but they do not make a person a Sufi. From the perspective of *Taṣawwuf*, forms are secondary. Those who seek the wisdom of Sufism concern themselves with essence.

Students of the Naqshbandī-Mujaddidī Order, for example, typically live in the world like other members of society—working, raising families, and sharing in the normal responsibilities of daily life. At the same time, they engage in practices which support their spiritual growth. It is not a question of choosing between the spiritual life and the worldly life. If that were required, then the student who did not reach the destination might think, "If I hadn't wasted my time with this path, by now I would be known and respected in society, I would be married and have children, I would hold a good job or run my own business!" With successful involvement in "worldly" work, if (God forbid) a student does not reach the destination, he or she will have no such regrets.

Those who aspire to plumb the depths of Sufism can benefit from striving to find the middle path in all circumstances. In the Qur'ān, Islam is described as *a middle nation* or *a community of the middle way*.[21] The Sufi aspirant applies this principle by avoiding extremism in all aspects of his or her thoughts, actions, and speech. In diet, he or she will typically eat moderately, avoiding both gluttony and constant fasting. In exercising authority, he or she will reserve whatever power he or she may have, using it wisely and only when necessary. In upholding right conduct, he or she will eschew both the extreme rigidity that imposes fixed standards on everyone, and the extreme liberality that allows each person to define his or her own standards. In these and other respects, the disciple of Sufism operates from a place of equanimity and balance.

Most contemporary societies place little credence in moderation. People find it easier to be extreme in their attitudes and actions, as evidenced in realms ranging from consumer spending to politics. They see no value in striving perpetually to safeguard one's affinity to God through obligatory prayers or other such acts. Consuming, socializing, and competing for wealth and success are considered mainstays of life. Renunciation may be commendable—even the sign of a spiritually advanced soul—but it is not "normal."

Those few individuals who do adopt renunciation are as prone to extremism as everyone else. While their peers over-indulge in materialism, they indulge in self-denial, subjecting themselves to the pangs of austere hunger and thirst.

It is actually easier to live alone in a cave and do nothing but spiritual practices than to lead a normal, responsible life, fulfilling necessary duties while maintaining spiritual practices. Generally travelers on the Sufi path choose the latter way, for they have found that the balanced, middle course is most conducive to refinement of the soul.

***

Question 18: Students' Attainments Past and Present

Can students today achieve the same degree of insight as those of previous centuries?

I mentioned that in earlier times, students would withdraw from the world, eat little, and curtail their social interactions. They would renounce everything except God, and their hearts would become so polished that they could see the essence of all matters. If you, like they, were to turn away from worldly life, retreat to a mountain or monastery, and take little food, you too might begin to have visions and extraordinary powers. But modern-day students cannot and are not asked to do this; and in any case, visions and extraordinary powers are not the goal.

Living as ordinary members of society, seekers today may find it difficult to polish the heart to the same degree as those who came before. But they have the potential to do so. If, in addition to fulfilling their worldly responsibilities, they are regular and punctual in their practices, devoting four to six hours daily to meditation and other aspects of the study, then I expect that one day, they will reach the highest degrees of enlightenment. God responds to sincerity. God is merciful and does not allow the efforts of any person to be in vain. The Prophet Muhammad ﷺ reported that God revealed, "If My servant draws near to Me an arm's length, I draw near to My servant a fathom's length. If My servant comes to Me walking, I run toward My servant" (Ḥadīth Qudsi[22]).

Consider what scientists have accomplished through their strenuous efforts to control nature. They have sent astronauts to the moon; now they aspire to travel to Mars and beyond. In contrast, spiritually-inclined individuals have been sleeping rather than exerting themselves. They have not been as diligent as either their predecessors in *Taṣawwuf* or their contemporaries in other disciplines. Consequently, the door of spirituality has remained closed.

Today we think it impossible to achieve that which was possible for previous generations. But I assure you, if young people come forward, show courage and consistency, and apply themselves to the field of spirituality, we may witness the same or even better results than we did in the past.

***

Question 19: The Length of the Journey

How long does the journey take?

The time required depends on the ability and capacity of the seeker. Talents differ, so it is difficult to propose a fixed time frame. Look at it this way. If I put a flame to dry wood, it will ignite easily and burn well, giving off warmth and light. If I put the flame to green, wet wood, it will not burn. It will sputter, hiss, and make a lot of smoke! However much we may want wet wood to burst into flame, it cannot; it is simply not its nature. It has to season, and seasoning (as the word implies) takes time. Just how much time, we cannot say for sure. Only God knows.

This is the correct answer, but when I give it to my students, I often detect that they are dissatisfied. Let me say, then, that if a seeker is sincere, conscientious, and regular in the practices, approximately seven to ten years are needed to attain selflessness. But this is only the beginning. There are levels and then more levels. The journey continues until one's last breath. If one is not fulfilled even then, God's grace and mercy will carry one to completion.

***

Question 20: Group Study

Do your students engage in group practices? What guidelines would you suggest for study groups?

In earlier times, students who were accepted for training would reside together, with their shaykh, in a *khānaqāh* or *takīyah* (Sufi study center[23]). The shaykh stayed in one place, and students gathered around him. Now such arrangements are rare. A hundred years ago, people went to the well for water; today, pipes bring water to our homes. So, too, many seekers once traveled long distances to be with shaykhs, but now, shaykhs travel from place to place meeting with seekers. As a result, students of the same shaykh frequently meet in small groups in various locations, rather than living and studying all together in a spiritual community.

I encourage students who live near each other to meet regularly and to form a common brotherhood and sisterhood in support of their spiritual pursuits. However, the Naqshbandī-Mujaddidī methods are internal and personal, not external or social. A typical group meeting includes performing the evening or nighttime *ṣalāh* (prayer) together, and then spending most of the time sitting, in silence, with each person doing his or her assigned recitations and meditation.

Although outwardly uneventful, these group meditations play an important role in students' progress. Sitting with others magnifies the blessings that a seeker receives from the practices. It is fine to meditate alone; but the student gains more from meditating with others, for everyone in the group benefits from the blessings coming to each individual. Suppose you invite a friend to join you in paying a visit to relatives. When you reach your relatives' home, they serve tea and sweets. Naturally, you are not the only one to enjoy this hospitality. Your friend also shares in it. Analogously, in a group, different kinds of blessings flow to each student, and the benefits of all these blessings carry over to everyone in the gathering. Because those who take part in group sittings receive more blessings, they progress more quickly.

An additional advantage of group meditation is that energy passes from one person to another. An atmosphere arises which has a soothing effect. In daily life, we each encounter a variety of people, some of whom exude darkness. At times, we may absorb this darkness: it stays with us even after we part from the person who affected us, even after we return home. Such darkness may accumulate in the course of several days to the point that we become unable to meditate. But attending a group meeting will dispel it. After meditating with others, we leave the company refreshed, with new enthusiasm and courage. We return home free of darkness and able to resume our spiritual pursuits.

Do you establish any guidelines for participating in study groups?

The *khānaqāhs* and *takīyahs* of the past were governed by rules and regulations formulated by shaykhs to promote their students' growth. While the format of Sufi groups has changed, some essential principles still apply. Two or three guidelines in particular can avert many problems.

In the material world, almost all groups, regardless of size, are characterized by an ongoing struggle for power. In spiritual groups, this should not be the case. The main object of a spiritual group is the purification of the heart, and its members should get together and stay together for this sole purpose.

How can a group attain harmony? One important guideline is to act as brothers and sisters, linked by the bond to a common teacher. Serving one another as siblings establishes the foundation for good relations. From a conscious attitude of brotherhood and sisterhood, love and affection emerge. The story is told that two children, a boy and a girl, grew up calling each other brother and sister, although they were not related by blood. When they were of marriageable age, their parents said that they were a perfect match and should wed. The boy refused. "All our lives, I have treated the woman you wish me to marry as a sister, and she has regarded me as her brother. With such an attitude between us, how could we marry? Besides, the affection we share could not be made greater through marriage."

A second important guideline is that group members should accept their own shortcomings. Each student should see any difficulty as his or her own fault, rather than someone else's. Let's say, for example, that one of your acquaintances attends a group meeting or otherwise expresses interest in Sufism, but he or she is not motivated enough to persevere, and soon drops the study. You should not blame that person, but rather attribute his or her withdrawal to your own shortcomings. Similarly, if conflict arises between you and someone else in the group, you should yield, take responsibility for the confrontation, and attribute its causes to your own flaws. After that, the matter is closed.

Another important watchword is humility. The secret of the greatest success lies in taking the least position. You should feel that even a dog in the shaykh's alley is better than you. Guard against the thought that by pursuing the path, you will one day become a shaykh. Focus on mastering self-refinement, not on attaining *ijāzah* (authorization to teach). Guiding others is an immense responsibility. A powerful caliph once said, "Had I been a blade of grass, I would have nothing to account for. But as a man of office, I must account for much." Please do not think that becoming a shaykh is easy. It is very difficult. Even if people try to convince you to teach, you should decline, saying, "I'm not fit for that." Pursue the path for purification, not for status.

***

Question 21: Sufi Practices in Daily Life

How can aspirants translate the Sufi practices into daily life? How much importance is placed on trying to do this?

Simply doing the Sufi practices regularly and sincerely cultivates qualities such as compassion, patience, contentment, equanimity, and selflessness. The inner growth of these qualities manifests outwardly as *adab* (spiritual courtesy).

Students automatically translate the benefits of the path into their daily activities by centering their lives around meditation, prayer, *dhikr* (remembrance), and *sharī'ah* (religious or sacred law). In Islam, there is only *tawḥīd* (unity). Life is not separated into "work" and "spiritual pursuits" except in the mind of the individual. This division is an illusion that emerges from conditioning based on duality. Sufism is holistic. Every act and decision of the student can and should reflect knowledge gained on this path.

To accept and be accepted as a student is an honor. You have heard the saying, "My word is my bond." If you have pledged to pursue the Sufi path, you have forged a bond, and at all times you should be conscious of the commitment you have made. Strive to remember who, why, and where you are until this awareness pervades every action. Eventually, everything you touch, say, and do will be permeated by your gratitude for this opportunity and by the strength and wisdom you have gained from it.

The journey begins with practicing. Its effects expand as the student continues to practice, extending service and kindness to others, praying to the Almighty, and allowing his or her sincerity to come forward.

Although the mind may demand a complex explanation, none is necessary. This is not a complicated formula. The seeker holds to his or her commitment no matter what the circumstances, and step by step, the process and its results become clear.

***

Question 22: Qualities Developed by the Aspirant

Would you please describe the nature of the individual who has attained the goal of Sufism?

Although it is difficult to generalize about those who have reached the destination of the Sufi path, let me at least summarize some of the qualities to which those who travel the path may aspire.

One quality of the Sufi is that he or she has connected himself or herself with God. He or she has become certain about the Almighty—not just certain that there is a higher power behind all existence, but conscious of the Supreme Power within and around us. The Sufi sees the hand of the Almighty in every arrangement, and perceives how the management of this universe is under God's direction.

A Sufi sees a personal relationship with God in every human being, every living thing, and every element in nature. The Divine Presence is not somewhere far removed from us, nor is it something to which only a select few can draw near. Rather, it is close to us, around us, within us. We read in the Qur'ān that *God is with you wherever you may be*[24] and *God is nearer to you than your jugular vein.*[25]

A traditional teaching story tells of a young fish who turns to his elder and says, "I've heard rumors in school about something called water. I'm sure it's a myth. They say it's everywhere, but how can it be, when I've never noticed it? Can you help me see it?" The elder replies, "No, I cannot help you see it. But I can tell you that if it were *not* here, you would certainly be aware of its absence." Like fish in water, we are all living in the Divine Presence, drinking it, breathing through it. Those who pursue the Sufi path strip away the veil of illusion and separation so that they may see clearly their origin and state. They become aware of the Divine Presence and expressive of the Divine Attributes that surround and are within us.

To the Sufi, God is caretaker, friend, and beloved. The Sufi knows that God is involved in all personal affairs. Whatever transpires is in accordance with God's wishes. You may find the Sufi to be optimistic, cheerful, happy, contented with simply going about his or her work, confident that everything will be all right. The Sufi sees beyond the external and apparent, and trusts that there is a purpose and meaning to all circumstances. He or she develops the perceptive organs of consciousness necessary to gain understanding of that meaning.

Islam, like many other religions, affirms that there is life after death. The Sufi does not merely accept this as a religious tenet, but is able to feel or taste its truth. He or she is acutely aware of the need to prepare for the hereafter during this life. Not knowing when he or she will die, he or she takes great care to utilize time fully, striving to remember God with whatever time is left and to entrust all other matters to God. Rabi'ah (r.a.), the famous saint and teacher of Basra, said, "O God, my whole occupation and all my desire in this world, of all worldly things, is to remember Thee, and in the world to come, of all things of the world to come, is to meet Thee. This is on my side, as I have stated; now do Thou whatsoever Thou wilt."[26]

The Sufi has subjugated or overcome self interest. Again I quote Rabi'ah (r.a.), who said, "O God, if I seek paradise or fear hell, give me neither."[27] The Sufi is motivated neither by the desire for bliss nor by dread of punishment. Similarly, he or she does not act in order to earn praise or be labeled a "good" or "spiritual" person. A spiritual dimension has developed within the Sufi such that he or she seeks out truth for the sake of truth, works for the sake of the work, and practices kindness for the sake of kindness, compassion for the sake of compassion, forgiveness for the sake of forgiveness.

The Sufi also maintains an attitude of *iḥsān*: to act as if one is seeing God everywhere, and if one does not see Him, to know that He is seeing or watching one. *Iḥsān* implies both the pursuit of excellence and an awe of God. The Sufi respects God as the Ultimate Truth, and he or she understands that within God's creation, certain things are expected of each individual—as a human being, a parent, a seeker, a student, a friend, a professional, and so on. He or she is always mindful of the obligation to fulfill these responsibilities, to do what he or she has been prepared to do, holding nothing back but rather trusting fully in God. The Sufi strives to perfect whatever he or she does, not to achieve some material goal, but because God has given each of us the way, the blessing, and the responsibility for our own perfection.

The Sufi has learned to be in the right place at the right time. He or she dedicates himself or herself to undertaking the action appropriate to each moment, having considered the situation and circumstances. According to the Central Asian mystic Andakī (r.a.) (d. 1157), "Effort is not effort without *zamān, makān, ikhwān* (right time, right place, right companions)."

The Sufi is a servant. Although he or she may be a master in terms of teaching others, his or her mastery comes from loving service. Service is a necessary means through which knowledge is expressed and the purpose of human life is fulfilled. Khwaja Yūsuf Hamadānī (r.a.) (d. 1140), one of the foremost Central Asian masters of wisdom, said, "Service to humanity is not just helpful to correct living. By its means the inner knowledge can be preserved, concentrated, and transmitted." Sufis typically are not pietists, especially in this day and age. Striving to be "in the world and not of the world," the Sufi attends to professional, domestic, and social duties, and then late at night or early in the morning sits in meditation. He or she is an ordinary person with extraordinary capabilities.

A Sufi said, "Our hearts are with the beloved Creator, but our hands are busy in the world with what we are to do." This quality is described as "solitude amidst the crowd." While in the world, the Sufi preserves inner solitude by turning to God. Whatever worldly affair engages the Sufi, he or she tries to perform it humbly, with trustworthiness, righteousness, and goodness. This attitude transforms the work into *'ibādah* (service to God).

Often the Sufi goes unrecognized by society. In contrast to the person who seeks power and fame under the guise of spirituality, the Sufi may keep a low profile. He or she focuses on fulfilling his or her work, and on encouraging the development of those around him or her using the most effective, legitimate means available.

***

Question 23: Transferring Sufism to the West

Have you encountered any challenges in transferring Sufi methods from India to the West?

The methods have proven their effectiveness. Our particular order emphasizes quality more than quantity. The applicability of the teachings is measured not by numbers of students, but by the results among those who use the methods as they were intended to be used.

In every instance, one should hope for the best. I must admit, however, that I have been a little discouraged by the attitudes and expectations that some Westerners bring to the path. They seem to be interested in a kind of spiritual materialism—what I call "spiritualism"—rather than spirituality. They seek peace of mind, power, phenomena, fame, or fortune as a result of doing spiritual exercises, rather than the results of a true search for the Holy Essence. Although many Westerners sense the importance of meditation and contemplation, many also are unwilling to undergo the discipline in the fold of an authentic tradition. This discipline alone can guarantee their access to the joy attained through contemplation of the celestial realities.

Rather than applying themselves to any one spiritual path, Westerners often taste many paths. Having once tried a path (no matter how briefly), they assume that they are qualified to judge it. Is it any wonder that so many seekers turn to self-realization centers, pseudo-masters from the East, unauthorized practices, and even mind-altering drugs?

In Sufism, the student's relationship to the teacher is of utmost importance. He or she must submit completely to make real progress. Yet, Westerners are wary of the term "submission." They fear that to submit means to lose one's identity and compromise one's freedom. People become so ensconced in their own ideas of freedom and individuality that they fail to see the benefits of real inner liberation and of taking personal responsibility for the choices they make. When one truly adopts the path, one is no longer "free" in the sense of being unaccountable, undisciplined, and unresponsive to guidance. Rather, one discovers new levels of freedom and identity that are inherent in trust and faith.

Unfortunately, it is difficult to find Westerners who are able to make a commitment and adhere to this path long enough to make this discovery. Their whole ego structure becomes threatened, driving them away. Often people become arrogant and challenge the value of trusting and respecting another human being completely, particularly one from a different culture. The ego tells the prospective student, "That person does not understand me or my culture. Therefore, he or she cannot know what is best for me."

In some cases, the ego asserts itself by convincing the aspirant that he or she is qualified to teach, and that the teacher simply is failing to recognize his or her level of spiritual attainment. I must say that the desire to become a teacher, shaykh, or guru puzzles me. I believe it reflects a uniquely Western interpretation of individuality. In the East, the average person feels no conflict between his or her individuality and his or her membership as one among equals in a group. In the West, many people equate individuality with standing out. They define themselves on the basis of being special, superior, or more knowledgable (and therefore "right"). This tendency may lead students to desire titles of authority, without regard for the qualifications needed to carry them out.

I have also found that attitudes toward personal relationships and family life can impede spiritual progress. According to Western culture, romantic relationships are a key to fulfillment. Often, romance is pursued at all costs, even if this means sacrificing other goals or accomplishments. Couples that have been married for years and even raised children together may divorce simply because the "spark" has gone out of their relationship. Similarly, couples are wedding on the basis of romantic attraction, without considering partners' spiritual needs. An individual who feels strong inner yearnings may marry a person who feels none, even though such a match will probably stunt his or her spiritual growth. The likelihood of such mismatches (and the degree of distraction from one's practices!) increases when men and women engage in sexual relations before marrying. For the true seeker, marriage must be based not only on attraction, but on spiritual compatibility and on a shared commitment to supporting one another in maintaining the practices and duties of the student.

***

PART 2: IN-DEPTH EXPLORATIONS AND TECHNICAL EXPLANATIONS

Question 24: Islam's Role in the Path of the Sufi

Is it necessary to embrace Islam in order to do the Sufi practices? Islam is not only an alien religion to me, but is, as I understand it, associated with a culture and way of life totally different from my own.

I should premise my answer by pointing out that as a Muslim, I bring an Islamic perspective to your question. I understand why you raise it, but I also understand the benefits of being Muslim. However, Sufism is not designed to propagate religion; its purpose is to promote an experience of nearness to God.

Islam today is often confused with customs, political movements, and extremist views that use its name without upholding its principles. Splinter groups within Islamic communities have preached intolerance and dogmatism, fueling stereotypes. While many non-Muslims are now striving to deepen their understanding of Islam, others have slipped into equating Islam with oppression and terrorism.

To better understand Islam, we can start with the word itself. The word *islam* comes from the Arabic root *s-l-m*, derivatives of which mean surrender, submission, peace, safety, security, wholeness, and well-being. None of these definitions imply the institutional structure, hierarchy, or dogma that is typically ascribed to religion. They point instead to the human potential to achieve inner peace, wholeness, and security through being conscious and aware in the Presence of the Divine. The teachings revealed by God to the Prophet Muhammad ﷺ offer a framework for deepening the relationship between individuals and their Creator throughout moment-to-moment life.

The term *islam* describes the reverent submission to God that all Divinely-inspired religions enjoin and evoke. The Prophet Muhammad himself 🕮 said that he did not bring a new message, but rather affirmed the message that gave rise to Judaism, Christianity, and other faiths.

Every religious system has two parts: *dīn* (the essential principles of belief) and *sharī'ah* (religious or sacred law). *Dīn* has remained the same in all ages, for its guidance is universal and timeless. All religions based on revelation offer the same *dīn*, consisting of two fundamentals: submission to the will of God (*islam*), Who is One (monotheism, or *tawḥīd* in Arabic); and good actions (*al-'amal aṣ-ṣālih*). According to the Qur'ān, God sent every civilization a messenger conveying this *dīn*.[28]

In contrast, *sharī'ah*—the body of law governing the expression of *dīn* in daily life and worship—has changed with time and place. The Indian theologian Shāh Walīullāh (r.a.) (d. 1762) noted that God guided the prophets[29] to present aspects of *sharī'ah* that reflected the needs of their communities. The *sharī'ah* or law brought by Noah 🕮 suited his society. God revealed additional laws to Moses 🕮, addressing his people's circumstances. The teachings of Jesus 🕮 refined *sharī'ah* for his day and age. The progressive revelation of *sharī'ah* reached completion with Muhammad 🕮, the final prophet.[30]

The *sharī'ahs* of Islam, Judaism, and Christianity differ regarding such matters as the prescribed forms of prayer, charity, and fasting. Islam, being least familiar in the West, is most likely to be perceived as alien; but the beliefs underlying its rituals confirm truths familiar to people of faith throughout history.

The Islamic attestation of faith (*kalīmah*) consists of two phrases: *lā ilāha illāllāh* and *Muḥammadun rasūl Allāh. Lā ilāha illāllāh*—"there is no god but God"—summarizes *dīn*, the monotheism shared by all Divinely-inspired religions. *Muḥammadun rasūl Allāh* means "Muhammad is the Messenger of God." With this statement, the Muslim accepts the *sharī'ah* brought by the Prophet Muhammad ﷺ.

Followers of other monotheistic faiths have no trouble agreeing with *lā ilāha illāllāh,* for they already believe in only one God. *Muḥammadun rasūl Allāh* poses a greater challenge. To accept Muhammad ﷺ as one of God's messengers contradicts lessons taught to many non-Muslims in childhood. In addition, the guidelines of Islamic *sharī'ah* differ from the customs and norms of Western societies.

It is natural, therefore, for non-Muslims to ask whether a person must embrace Islam to do the Sufi practices.

All sacred paths lead to the Ultimate Reality, and progress along any of these authentic ways is progress toward the destination. For this reason, I tell my students that the seeker who wishes to adopt the path of Christianity, Judaism, or any other revealed religion is free to do so.

Some seekers, disenchanted with religious institutions, question the need to practice any religion at all. To this question, I would reply that despite the plentiful flaws of institutions and leaders, religious teachings still provide guidance for the spiritual search. Moses عليه السلام, Jesus عليه السلام, and Muhammad ﷺ did not just talk about laws and rituals: they helped their followers achieve a deeper, more intimate relationship with the Divine. For those who strive to become God-conscious, the prophets' teachings remain as relevant today as ever.

It is true that individuals may progress toward realizing God without any religion or structure. Everybody can sit in contemplation and sense the Divine Presence; no particular practice is necessary. However, without applying the guidance that God made available through religions, it is difficult to go beyond intuitive awareness to actually make contact with the Almighty. At a certain point, most people recognize that they need help, and turn for assistance to religious and spiritual teachers and teachings.

Why do individuals on the Sufi path find this assistance within Islam? Why not in some other religion? The answer is twofold. First, the student of Sufism does not choose Islam any more than a child chooses its parents or genetic makeup. Sufism arose as an Islamic discipline, in much the same way that the Benedictine, Franciscan, and Dominican Orders arose as expressions of Christianity. There is no Sufism other than Islamic Sufism. Any mystical practice cut off from its source in revealed religion will lose vitality, just as any tree cut from its roots will die.

Second, according to Sufi teachings, the progressive stages of *sharī'ah* are a succession of vehicles, each useful in its own era. In the time of Moses عليه السلام, the most effective vehicle for spiritual progress was the *sharī'ah* he taught. In the time of Jesus Christ عليه السلام, his *sharī'ah* was most effective. Six hundred years later, the Prophet Muhammad ﷺ was guided by God to introduce a *sharī'ah* that superseded that of Jesus عليه السلام. Because Muhammad ﷺ was the final prophet, Sufi masters regard his *sharī'ah* as the most up-to-date vehicle, best suited to the needs of contemporary seekers.

Of course, we cannot expect all non-Muslims with an interest in Sufi practices to become Muslims. To impose such a demand would be inconsistent with Islam, a natural way of life with teachings that acknowledge the difficulties inherent in switching religions. No one can impose a belief system on a person who does not incline toward it from within. The

Qur'ān states, *Let there be no compelling in religion.*[31] The Prophet Muhammad ﷺ said, "Do not bring into religion the hardness created by human beings."

The first Sufi teachers in the West, recognizing non-Muslims' doubts about Islam, introduced Sufism as a universal religion. Certain schools of Sufism flourished on the basis of universalism; to this day, they perpetuate brands of so-called Sufism with no foundation in Islam.

Sufism cannot exist outside Islam, and those who assert its independence lead others down a dead-end track. Teaching methods are needed that acknowledge the link between Sufism and Islam while introducing non-Muslims to the practices. Sufi teachings can benefit anyone. Yet seekers should also be aware that there are many levels to these teachings and many decisions a person must make in the process of pursuing them. The specific teachings on meditation that my institute offers are divided into three levels, or phases. Seekers of any religion can complete the first and second phases, which develop the faculties of the heart. The third phase requires students to dive deeper into Islam. Students come to understand from experience the relationship between applying the Sufi practices and relating as a Muslim to the Qur'ān and the *ḥadīth* (recorded sayings and actions of the Prophet ﷺ), observing the five daily prayers, and otherwise embracing Islam.

Islam cannot be seen just as a religion. It is a way of life. Much of the depth of Islam is realized in the heart. Sometimes as students experience firsthand the insights available through Sufism, they are drawn to know more about its foundations. Some discover the meaning of *lā ilāha illāllāh, Muḥammadun rasūl Allāh* for themselves. But always this is at their own pace, based on their own evolving understanding.

The Prophet Muhammad ﷺ had a staunch opponent named Abū Sufyān. After years of persecuting the Muslims (and just before the Muslims took over his city), Abū Sufyān finally had a change of heart. He came to the Prophet ﷺ to profess faith. He said, "I have no doubts regarding the first part of the *kalīmah—lā ilāha illāllāh.* But I still question the second part—*Muḥammadun rasūl Allāh.*"

The Prophet ﷺ indicated that by reciting the first part of the *kalīmah* with conviction, Abū Sufyān had joined the community of Muslims. He also expressed confidence that, God willing, Abū Sufyān's questions regarding the second part of the *kalīmah* would disappear in time. He then asked his own uncle to house Abū Sufyān overnight.

Abū Sufyān had never before seen the Muslim community from within. He knew of the Muslims' faith and devotion, but had not witnessed the power of their practices. That evening and the following morning, he observed the Muslims at prayer. He noted the companions' affection for their leader, and their leader's concern for them. Adding these observations to his own experience of the Prophet's charity, justice, and forgiveness, Abū Sufyān recognized the Prophet ﷺ for what he was.

Abū Sufyān asked for a second meeting. This time he declared loudly, "Muhammad is a true prophet!" Weeping, he professed the second part of the *kalīmah* and embraced Islam with the most sincere of hearts.

The Sufi practices bring individuals closer to God. Students who choose to become Muslims are eligible for the full range of practices, which, in association with the Islamic way of life, foster profound internal transformation. Students who choose not to embrace Islam may nevertheless find that even the preliminary practices enhance their knowledge of themselves, their relationship with God, their understanding of Divine will, and their faith.

***

Question 25: Sources of Sufism

What are the sources of Sufism? Some people think it originated in philosophies or religions outside of Islam. What is your understanding?

Orientalists have expressed various opinions concerning the origins of Sufism. Some authors argue that it was influenced by Greek philosophy. To support this hypothesis, Professor R.A. Nicholson of Cambridge cited similarities between the works of Sufis and Greek philosophers. Other authors have asserted that Sufism derives from Vedanta or Buddhism. In my view, all these theories are mistaken. While some of the movements' principles are similar, similarities do not prove that one movement comes from another. Professor Louis Massignon, a leading French scholar of Islamic mysticism, concluded after extensive study that Sufism originated in the Holy Qur'ān and the traditions of the Prophet Muhammad ﷺ. It was not transplanted from outside, but rather originated in Islam.[32]

The Indian scholar Shāh Walīullāh (r.a.) (d. 1762) observed that the methods adopted by various orders conformed to the natural inclinations of people in the areas where these orders arose. Shaykhs may have drawn on certain aspects of other religions or systems, particularly when customs had become so deeply rooted as to be unassailable. But we should avoid reading too much into superficial similarities. A Sufi aspirant sitting in meditation looks much like a yogi sitting in meditation, but the two differ significantly in their methods and purposes.

On another level, the question of which mysticism derives from what source is academic. The mystic impulse exists within each human soul. Certain principles have found expression in every country, every language, every religion—not because societies borrow from one another, but because God created us with an inborn yearning to know the Divine. It is human nature to turn toward spiritual improvement and training. If concepts and practices found in Sufism are found also in Christianity, Judaism, Hinduism, Buddhism, and other traditions, it does not mean they are un-Islamic, any more than they are un-Christian, un-Judaic, un-Hindu, or un-Buddhist. They are legitimately claimed by all faiths, for they reflect the human condition. Those who miss this point—who insist on establishing external sources for Sufism or other spiritual traditions—miss both the uniqueness of each monument of human discovery, and the unity that underlies all creation.

***

Question 26: Sufi Orders (*Ṭarīqahs*)

Who were the first Sufis? You have referred to various orders. How did these come into being, and what is their importance?

In all times and places, there have been individuals whose deep yearning and inner restlessness have drawn them to spend time in meditation, prayer, or retreat. Such a person was the Prophet Muhammad ﷺ, who—even before he began receiving revelations—periodically withdrew to a cave outside of Mecca to devote himself to worshipping God.

Later, as the early community of Muslims emerged, some among his companions likewise inclined toward the deepest possible expression and fulfillment of their love for God.[33] The Qur'ān states, *Verily your Lord knows that you [Muhammad] keep vigil nearly two-thirds of the night, and sometimes half of it or a third of it, you and a group of those that are with you....*[34]

The guidance that forms the basis for the Sufis' practices is found in the Qur'ān and in the teachings of the Prophet ﷺ. For example, the practice of silently invoking the Divine (*dhikr khafī*) was first taught by the Prophet ﷺ to his close friend Abū Bakr ؓ (d. 634 C.E.) as the two sought refuge in a cave during the *hijrah*, or emigration from Mecca to Medina.[35] The Sufi practice of invoking God aloud (*dhikr jalī*) may be traced to guidance given by the Prophet ﷺ to his son-in-law 'Alī ؓ (d. 661 C.E.).[36] The *miraj* or night journey of the Prophet ﷺ has long inspired mystics as a metaphor for the spiritual path. The Prophet ﷺ was taken by God from Mecca to Jerusalem, and from Jerusalem was carried through the seven heavens, finally coming to within two bows' length of God. So, too, the Sufi aspirant strives to transcend the limitations of space and time and to draw near to the Divine.[37]

These and other examples indicate a strong mystical element in the life of the Prophet Muhammad ﷺ and the early community of Muslims. However, the term "Sufism" does not seem to have been used to describe the spiritual dimension of Islam until many years later.

The emergence of the first individuals to be labeled "Sufis" is commonly linked to historical developments of the seventh and eighth centuries. Between 622 and 632 C.E., the Holy Prophet ﷺ established in Medina a society that reflected Islamic principles of equity, justice, consensus, piety, and sensitive leadership. After his lifetime, the first four caliphs ؓ followed his guidance, governing the Muslims' rapidly expanding territories in accordance with the teachings of the Qur'ān and the *sunnah* (example and guidance of the Prophet ﷺ).

Following the assassination of 'Alī ؓ in 661 C.E., Muslim governments began to stray from the *sunnah*. The Umayyad dynasty (661-749 C.E.) abolished the consensus-based system of selecting caliphs, replacing it with hereditary rule. It put an end to the open, equitable relations between common people and leaders that had distinguished the pious caliphs. Politics became mostly divorced from piety and religion. Leaders were no longer specifically chosen for their spiritual insight, but often rose to power through intrigue and violence. The cohesion of the Muslim community was destroyed, and with it, the Muslims' unity of purpose.

Within a hundred years after the *hijrah*, leadership of the Muslim community had passed out of the hands of its most devout members. Various subgroups observed that instead of upholding the *dīn* (the essential principles of faith), their rulers had become immersed in worldly affairs and selfish ends. Many well-known and respected Muslims severed relations with the government altogether.

In the second century after the *hijra*, some of those who rejected the secular government started to be called Sufis. The Persian shaykh Abū Hāshim Kūfi (r.a.) (d. about 776) was the first person to be known by this name. Between approximately 660 and 850 C.E., the earliest Sufi circles emerged, reflecting devout Muslims' opposition to the degeneration of leadership.

The second phase in the spread of Sufi teachings coincides with another important period of Islamic history, from

850 C.E. until the tenth century. Greek philosophy and sciences had become current among Muslims, and Islamic society was faced with the storm of rationalism. The common people found their beliefs shaken to the core. Doubts assailed them. As reason and worldliness threatened to displace faith, Muslims became anxious, confused, and disheartened. Finally, Sufi masters raised a voice of protest against Greek philosophy. To counteract its influence, they stressed the doctrine of *'ishq* (passionate love) and the experiences attained through spiritual states of the heart.

The third stage in the development of Sufism took place in the tenth century C.E. Using their tongues in speech and their intellects in writing, the sages of this era tried to reawaken a religious spirit that would permeate people's day-to-day lives. They recognized that human behavior could not improve as long as human hearts were consumed with secular concerns. They emphasized purification of the self, guiding individuals to overcome worldly and rationalist conditioning. They helped people revivify their inner lives by providing a framework for ethical and moral outer lives.

During this period, Sufi teachings became widespread. Authoritative books were written and disseminated. A technical vocabulary developed. Groups were established, although they did not yet assume the form of the orders that we know today.

Between the tenth and twelfth centuries, Sufism became a widely respected discipline. Many great scholars and spiritual masters taught during this period, establishing the Sufi practices and terminology. Several *ṭarīqahs* (orders[38]) were founded.

By the end of the thirteenth century, Sufism had become a well-defined science of spiritual awakening. Through experimentation and investigation, Shaykhs had developed transferable techniques for self-refinement, the efficacy of which was confirmed by numerous aspirants. The Sufi *ṭarīqahs* had become the basis for a widespread mystical movement, lending new life to humanity's age-old spiritual quest. Teachers such as the Persian scholar Imām al-Ghazālī (r.a.) (d. 1111), Shaykh 'Abd al-Qādir Jīlānī of Baghdad (r.a.) (d. 1166), Shaykh Abū Ḥafs 'Umar Suhrawardī (r.a.) (d. 1234) (also of Baghdad), and the Andalucian master Ibn 'Arabī (r.a.) (d. 1240) provided complete explanations of the philosophy, practices, and goals of Sufism. Love for the Divine found expression and inspiration in such magnificent works as *The Walled Garden of Truth*, by Afghan poet Ḥakīm Ṣanā'ī (r.a.) (d. about 1150); *The Conference of the Birds*, by the Persian master Farīduddīn 'Aṭṭār (r.a.) (d.1230); and the *Divan-i Shams-i Tabrīzī* of Rūmī (r.a.) (d. 1273), founder of the Mevlevī order in Konya, Turkey. This period might be considered the golden age of Sufism.

So timeless and comprehensive were the teachings of this era that although Sufism passed through various stages of decline and reform in subsequent centuries, its philosophic knowledge and methodological foundations changed very little.

This historical overview gives you a sense of the context that gave rise to the various orders. Further details may be found in the many books that address their histories.[39] Let me just briefly introduce several orders or chains of transmission (*silsilahs*) that you may wish to investigate further: the Khwājagān, Qādirī, Chishtī, Suhrawardi, Shādhilī, Naqshbandī, and Mujaddidī.

Silsilah Khwājagān developed in Turkestan. The best-known personalities of this order were Khwājah Aḥmad Yasawī (r.a.) (d. about 1167), a native of the area known today as China's Xinjiang Province, and Khwājah 'Abd al-Khāliq Ghujduwāni of Bukhara (r.a.) (d. 1179). The latter coined certain terms with special technical and spiritual meanings, and made the teachings of the order accessible and relevant to the people of his era. Khwājah Bahā'uddīn Naqshband (r.a.) (d. 1389), also of Bukhara, further advanced the understanding of Sufi thought.[40] The order subsequently took his name, Naqshbandī, and spread from Central Asia into India and Southeast Asia, Turkey, the Caucasus, the Middle East, the Balkans, and elsewhere.

Shaykh 'Abd al-Qādir Jīlānī (r.a.), born in 1077 C.E. in Jilan, Iran, mastered the scholarly disciplines of Islam before dedicating himself to austerities and spiritual studies as a young man. Eventually he settled in Baghdad (then the capital of the Muslim world), where his lectures routinely drew listeners by the thousands. He became an important public figure, overseeing charitable trusts, issuing judicial decisions, and addressing audiences that included high government officials. Themes he stressed included virtue, ethical conduct, and self-discipline. The popularity of his teachings continued after his death in 1166, inspiring his followers and subsequent generations of disciples to establish the Qādirī Order.

The Chishtī Order was founded by Shaykh Abū Is'ḥāq (r.a.) (d. 940 or 966). A native of Syria, Shaykh Abū Is'ḥāq was sent by his spiritual guide to teach in the town of Chisht (near Herat, Afghanistan). The order he established was later nourished and popularized by the eminent Shaykh Khwājah Moinuddīn Chishtī (r.a.) (d. 1236), originally of Iran, who studied and taught in Central Asia, Iraq, Arabia, and India. Known for his generosity, warmth, and compassion, Shaykh Moinuddīn Chishtī (r.a.) spread a message of peace and love. His commitment to service earned him the title "the one who shows kindness to the poor." Much of his later life was spent in Ajmer, India, which remains a major center of Chishtī teachings to this day.

The Suhrawardī Order originated in Baghdad under the guidance of Shaykh 'Abd al-Qādir Suhrawardī (d. 1168) and his nephew, Shaykh Abū Ḥafs 'Umar Suhrawardī (r.a.) (d. 1234). The latter authored *'Awārif al-ma'ārif* (*The Gifts of Gnosis*), a complete description of the administration of the *khānaqāh* (Sufi study center). The Suhrawardī Order differed from some others in its traditional interpretation of the *sharī'ah* (religious or sacred law). It also departed from more reclusive orders in playing an active role in government affairs, first in Persia and later in the Indian subcontinent, where the order flourished.

The Shādhilī Order derives its name from Shaykh Abū al-Ḥasan Shādhilī (r.a.) (d. 1258), a thirteenth-century Moroccan master who taught primarily in Egypt. Unlike some of his contemporaries, Shaykh Abu al-Ḥasan (r.a.) required that his students be well-educated in *sharī'ah* and have a skill or profession that would enable them to support their families and contribute to society.[41] The spiritual teachings of the Shādhilī Order spread across North Africa and into Arabia and Syria.

At the end of the sixteenth century, the Indian shaykh Aḥmad Farūqī Sirhindī (r.a.) (d. 1624) of the Naqshbandī Order reformed Sufism by boldly countering the doctrine of *waḥdat al-wujūd* (unity of being) with the doctrine of *waḥdat ash-shuhūd* (unity of being in vision).[42] He also reaffirmed the importance of *sharī'ah* in an effort to counteract the spread of un-Islamic practices among India's Muslims and Sufi circles. For this effort, he became known as the *Mujaddid-i alf-i thani*: "renewer of the second millennium." Due to the significance of his reforms to the

Naqshbandī teachings, his spiritual descendants became known as a new order, the Mujaddidī. Their teachings became popular throughout the Indian subcontinent, and spread eventually to the Caucasus, the Middle East, Asia Minor, and beyond.

These are but a few of the noteworthy chains of transmission and their founders. Countless other shaykhs have also contributed to the body of Islamic thought through their letters, writings, and philosophies. Today seekers look to all of these shaykhs for assistance on the journey.

Distinctions among orders are sometimes made on the basis of geographic origins or practices. By the ninth century C.E., differing methods had emerged among Sufi groups in northern Muslim lands (Persia, Turkestan, Afghanistan, and the Caucasus) and their counterparts to the south (in Arabia, Mesopotamia, Syria, Africa, and Spain). Southern *ṭarīqahs* typically preferred students to isolate themselves, give up worldly possessions, and entrust themselves wholly to the teacher. Northern *ṭarīqahs* more often encouraged students to continue to live and work in society and, while stressing the need for a shaykh, did not encourage veneration of shaykhs. In our era, *ṭarīqahs* that trace their origins to northern schools may employ concepts like "liberation," "self-annihilation," "permanent non-being," and "non-existence," whereas those originating from southern Sufis may be more concerned with union, love, manifestations, and visions. But these categories have never been rigid. Throughout history, shaykhs have mixed elements of various Sufi traditions.

In considering the *ṭarīqahs* today, one distinction still worth noting is that some orders emphasize verbal instruction, while others emphasize meditation and the imparting of instruction by transmission. A seeker may find teachings that employ one or the other approach (or combine both) most appropriate to his or her temperament and needs. However, all methods aim to bring students nearer to God. In the hands of a qualified shaykh, the varying techniques of the *ṭarīqahs* are like the surgeon's instruments: what matters to the person on the operating table is their role in restoring health, not the details of where they came from, who invented them, or how they compare to instruments in the room next door. Methods are means to the goal, not the goal itself. Ultimately, real and lasting benefits depend on the seeker's trust in God, in the Prophet ﷺ, and in his or her guide, for trust alone allows the seeker to put full attention into the practices assigned.

***

Question 27: Sufism's Role in Muslim Life

What do Muslims gain by practicing Taṣawwuf?

Sharī'ah is religious law, while *Taṣawwuf* and *ṭarīqah* (the mystical path) are its refinements and subtleties. When the Central Asian master Bahā'uddīn Naqshband (r.a.) (d. 1389) was asked (presumably by a Muslim) to define the purpose of Sufism, he replied, "It is to know in detail what you already know in brief." Not all people are inclined to go into such detail, nor does every person have the necessary aptitude. Muslims drawn to the path are those with an inquisitive nature who yearn to know the reality of existence and ardently wish to grasp the essence of *sharī'ah*.

As I have mentioned, Sufism deepens knowledge of the self, and from deepened self-knowledge comes greater understanding of God. Recognition of God's nearness can be achieved only after purification (*tazkīyah*) of the heart and self. Those who pursue the Sufi way focus on such purification, thereby developing *iḥsān*[43] : the capacity to be engrossed in prayer and other acts of worship "as if you are seeing God, and if you are not seeing God, knowing that God is seeing you." When a person becomes conscious, then imitative or deductive faith gives way to faith based on experience and witnessing.

This growth of faith (*īmān*) is enjoined upon Muslims by God. The Qur'ān makes clear that *islam* (submission to God) is one step, but becoming a *mu'min* (person of faith) is another. *The Bedouin Arabs say, "We have believed." Tell them, "You have not believed; rather say, 'We have become Muslims,' for faith has not yet found its way into your hearts."*[44]

Elsewhere in the Qur'ān, God states, *O you who believe! Believe in God....*[45] Muslims are encouraged to perfect their faith so that they may attain certainty of the Truth (*al Haqq*), which is the realization of God.

Sharī'ah (religious or sacred law) has three parts: knowledge, action, and sincerity of motive. The Muslim's challenge is to align all three. Sadly, we can observe some Muslims offering prayers, fulfilling the fast of Ramaḍān, paying *zakāh* (obligatory charity), and making the pilgrimage, but otherwise violating the values of Islam daily. These inconsistencies stem from inner impurities. The training provided by Sufism ennobles individuals, uprooting hypocrisy and other tendencies that stand in the way of living Islam.

Leading scholars of *sharī'ah* have acknowledged the importance of Sufism in refining faith. Imām Mālik ibn Anas (r.a.) (d. 795) of Medina, founder of the Mālikī *madh'hab*,[46] wrote, "[One] who practices *Taṣawwuf* without learning Sacred Law corrupts his faith, while one who learns Sacred Law without practicing *Taṣawwuf* corrupts himself. Only [the person] who combines the two proves true." Imām Aḥmad ibn Ḥanbal (r.a.) (d. 855), founder of the Baghdad-based Ḥanbalī *madh'hab*, said, "O my son, you have to sit with the people of Sufism, because they are like a fountain of knowledge, and they keep the remembrance of God in their hearts." Even Ibn Taymiyyah (d. 1328), a Syrian Muslim jurist known for his disapproval of Sufi teachings, wrote, "...some people criticized the people of *Sufiyyah* and *Taṣawwuf* and they said they were innovators, but the truth is, they are striving in God's obedience....So from them you will find the foremost in nearness by virtue of his striving."[47]

Today divisiveness racks Islam. It seems Muslims may already have fulfilled the prediction (often attributed to the Prophet Muhammad ﷺ) that their community would be fragmented into seventy-three sects. In the midst of turmoil, the only reliable foundation for a vital, comprehensive, and applicable Islam, capable of meeting the challenges of the modern world, lies in those people of faith who take Qur'ān to heart, not in academicians, leaders with narrow agendas, or proponents of rigidity and intolerance. The knowers of the heart of Islam have often been the Sufis. In their teachings, Muslims can discover the reality of Islam personally—and people of all religions can find hope that in the future, Islam will be identified globally with justice, service, and compassion.

***

Question 28: Initiations (*Bay'ah*)

Do you give initiations routinely, even to beginners?

The Indian shaykh Sayyid 'Abd al-Bāri Shah (r.a.) (d. 1900) once met Mawlvī Na'īm of Farangi Mahal in the city of

Lucknow. Mawlvī Na'īm asked if he regularly made others his disciples. Sayyid 'Abd al-Bāri Shah (r.a.) replied, "To be a *pīr* (shaykh) and make disciples is the habit of you and people like you. My concern is to take true seekers nearer to God." Mawlvī Na'īm accepted the gentle rebuke, saying, "This is God's favor, granted to whomsoever God wills."

In my capacity as a teacher, I travel to different places. If I come across someone seeking God's nearness, then with the *barakāt* (blessings) and help of the elders, I guide that person along the path as far as possible.

The relationship between shaykh and *murīd* or *murīda* (disciple) is variously interpreted in different cultures and orders. In India, the term "shaykh" often describes a spiritual healer who travels from town to town, meeting with people who come to request aid in their affairs. Through special prayers and curative and protective amulets (*tawiz*), he assists those who seek him out, and he receives payment in return. Within this context, many people become disciples of a sort. Most of them are contented with their limited connection to a shaykh. Neither they nor the shaykh expects that they will receive and perform assigned spiritual practices. This type of relationship is quite common.

The Naqshbandī-Mujaddidī Order views the bond between student and shaykh differently. The latter is a teacher, responsible for giving a full course of structured study and training in the spiritual life. Students or disciples are expected to commit to this study, just as they would to the course of study at a university. University students naturally expect their professor to have complete mastery of his or her subject. Similarly, disciples must have a trained and expert guide, whom they can trust completely and with whom they can learn and practice diligently.

Shaykhs of our particular order do not set out to attract large numbers of followers. We accept *bay'ah* (the pledge of initiation) only from those whom we find sincerely desirous of coming nearer to God.

The step of initiation is never taken at the outset. First, the ten *laṭā'if* (centers of consciousness) are awakened through preliminary exercises. Anyone is welcome to study up to this point. If a person then wishes to acquire deeper knowledge, he or she must give *bay'ah.*

Based on his experiences, Ḥazrat Sayyid 'Abd al-Bāri Shah (r.a.) disliked the system of making disciples (*pīr-i murīdi*). However, from a spiritual point of view, he deemed it necessary for students who had completed the initial exercises to become *murīds* or *murīdas* in order to establish a relationship (*rābiṭah*) with the shaykh conducive to further studies.

***

Question 29: Student-Teacher Relationship

Some people feel they can study Sufism without a teacher. Must everyone have a guide?

This is a significant question. To answer simply: whenever one embarks on a study, whatever it may be, the quickest way to learn is with the aid of a teacher. If one hopes to master advanced aspects of a field, one certainly needs a teacher.

In the spiritual *sulūk* (journey), some seekers are *murīds* and *murīdas* (disciples) and some are *murāds* (special individuals). *Murīds* and *murīdas* must find a teacher to guide them on the journey. There is a saying that if one has no shaykh, the devil becomes one's guide. Seekers who study independently are susceptible to being led astray by evil forces in the forms of their own desires, indolence, fears, or cravings for power. Satan intends that no one should take a step toward the Divine.

On rare occasions, an extraordinary individual may be so loved by God that God arranges directly for that person's training and guidance. Such individuals are known as *murāds*. Sometimes the mystic guide Khiḍr[48] ﷺ comes to the aid of the *murāds*. Sometimes the souls of the *awliyā'* (saints) assist them. However, the *murād* is as dependent on guidance as any other student. His or her relationship with the teacher differs only in its lack of physical form.

Because guidance from unseen sources may originate from the devil or one of his agents, any person who imagines himself or herself to be a *murād* should consult a living teacher. Only an authorized master can confirm the validity of such guidance.

In brief, everyone who wishes to pursue the spiritual journey stands in need of a teacher. One who chooses not to find a teacher risks being misled. I do not mean to deny that one can learn something on one's own, or to say that everyone who embarks on the search without a teacher will fail. But the seeker without a guide is in constant danger of not acting in accordance with the will of God and, consequently, of never reaching the final stage.

What are the respective roles of teacher and student in the Sufi learning process?

This question would take weeks to answer thoroughly. Allow me to address just a few important points.

In learning situations (as in many other contexts), aspects of the process sometimes get magnified out of proportion. Early in the development of Sufism, it became evident that one who wishes to pursue the path needs a teacher; but as time passed, the importance of the teacher received undue emphasis. In some instances, the role played by the Sufi master became more of a hindrance than a help. This has happened within almost all schools of Sufism at one time or another, due to the tendencies of unrefined human beings.

The shaykh is a guide: one qualified to teach because he or she has already gone through all the subtle aspects of the path that others wish to traverse. He or she is the authority responsible for leading the student to the right path. The student's role is to submit.

Westerners tend to misinterpret both authority and submission. Let's say I want to drive from Washington, D.C. to New York City. I do not know the way, so I hire a guide to come along and point out the route. Throughout the trip, the guide is the authority, and I submit without question to his or her expertise.

To what have I submitted—a human being? Only on one level, for on another level, the guide has simply directed me along pre-established routes, observing already-defined driving laws, to a destination that I myself specified. Sufism may appear to involve submission to another human being, but adherents of this path, like all Muslims, vest ultimate authority in God alone. The student takes direction from a shaykh, but he or she submits to God, not to a human being.

Accepting the shaykh's guidance ensures that the student's efforts bring him or her closer to the ultimate destination. Returning to our analogy: if I have a time-sensitive appointment in New York, then given my ignorance of the route, I would be foolish not to enlist a guide.

The seeker should choose a shaykh carefully, and after making that selection, pinpoint attention on the shaykh without diversion. Not to pay attention is like poison. Once when a student of the Naqshbandī Order was going to meet his shaykh, he encountered Khiḍr ﵇, yet passed him by without even a glance. The shaykh, upon seeing his student, realized by means of spiritual insight that he had walked right by Khiḍr ﵇. "You met such an important man and didn't even look at him?" the teacher queried. The student replied, "At the time, I was directing my attention toward you."

A second story tells of the Indian shaykh Khwājah Moinuddīn Chishtī (r.a.) (d. 1236). His deputy, Khwājah Quṭbuddīn Bakhtiyār Kākī (r.a.) (d. 1235), lived in Delhi. Moinuddīn Chishtī (r.a.) happened to visit Delhi, and all but one of the pupils of Bakhtiyar Kaki (r.a.) came to meet him. Moinuddīn Chishtī (r.a.) asked, "Has everybody come to meet me, or did someone stay behind?" Bakhtiyār Kākī (r.a.) replied, "Only one student remained behind, in his room. He's very weak and not able to come." Moinuddīn Chishtī (r.a.) said, "Since he cannot join us here, let's go to meet him there."

They went to the room of this man, whose name was Bābā Farīd (r.a.).[49] To rouse him, Bakhtiyār Kākī (r.a.) announced loudly, "See, my shaykh has come to see you. Stand up and greet him!" But Bābā Farīd (r.a.) laid his head on the feet of Bakhtiyār Kākī (r.a.). Without even casting his eyes on his shaykh's teacher, he said, "For me, O my shaykh, you are all in all."

In earlier times, once seekers had chosen a shaykh, they would sometimes put cloths in front of their eyes so as not to catch sight of anyone whom they might deem better than their shaykh. In this way, they avoided being assailed by the thought, "I wish I were that other person's student."

A seeker may knock at any door, as long as he or she has not selected one. But after choosing and being accepted by a shaykh, the student who hopes to succeed must observe the Sufi saying: "Hold on to that shaykh's door, and hold it fast."

Are there particular ways in which students express courtesy and respect toward the teacher?

The relationship of *murīd* and *murīda* to the shaykh is based on *adab* (spiritual courtesy). *Adab* has two parts: the first comprises formalities, and the second is of the heart. Centuries ago, students grasped *adab* fully and performed it in the spirit of the heart. If they were invited to a meeting or sought audience with the shaykh, they would enter his or her presence and stand, waiting patiently. If the shaykh did not speak to them, they did not mind. They realized that their teacher was busy with someone or something else from a spiritual point of view. So, there they stood. There is a purpose, a meaning behind such actions.

The spirit of *adab* is exemplified in another story of Khwājah Quṭbuddīn Bakhtiyār Kākī (r.a.). One day, he was taking a meal with a guest named Turkmān Biyābānī (r.a.). Bābā Farīd (r.a.) stood by to serve them. The two men ate with their hands from a common platter, in keeping with the custom of the time; but contrary to custom, Turkmān Biyābānī (r.a.) kept putting his hand under his armpit between bites. His host found this habit offensive, so Bābā Farīd (r.a.) signaled him to stop it.

Seeing Bābā Farīd's (r.a.) gesture, Turkmān Biyābānī (r.a.) raised his arm. Under his shoulder flowed a clear river. He said, "My respect and honor for Khwājah Quṭbuddīn Bakhtiyār Kākī (r.a.) is so great that I cannot put the hand that has been in my mouth back into his dish without washing it."

In those days, people realized the significance of such an act. Later, the spirit of *adab* decreased, but the outer forms remained. Today much of what passes for *adab* is mere formality, as students repeat rituals of courtesy with little awareness of their meaning. Such rituals are secondary to the natural, spiritual *adab* of the heart.

Adab of the heart develops along with knowledge, becoming more evident and consistent as the seeker learns and understands. When a baby spits, grabs, or turns its back on us, we do not get angry. But if a grown person acts in this manner, we take offense, because the adult knows better. So, too, as inner understanding grows, *adab* grows.

The essence of *adab* is to not divert one's attention from the shaykh. Even when one is facing the shaykh, one's attention may wander. Even when one is turned away, one can remain attentive. The secret of *adab* is to be attentive and attuned to the shaykh at all times, whether or not one is in the shaykh's presence.

Once when my shaykh was talking to me, I started thinking about my response. He reprimanded me, saying, "Are you listening? Or is your mind caught up in framing an answer?" My inattentiveness showed a lack of *adab*.

Adab can give rise to some delicate situations. It so happened that a teacher and a student were together on a cold night. When it came time to sleep, the student thought, "It's chilly tonight, and my shaykh may need some warm water when he wakes up." The student took a jug of water and held it on his chest to warm it for his shaykh. All night he stayed in this position, choosing not to sleep in order to look after the comfort of the shaykh. This is not formal *adab*, but *adab* of the heart.

It is also important that the student harbor no doubts about the teacher. If by chance a student has some misunderstanding which creates doubt, he or she should contact the teacher privately to try to express that misunderstanding.

At the same time, students must remember that every act of the teacher, large or small, has some hidden meaning. The teacher is always explaining and demonstrating the different points of spiritual instruction in his or her own way. The shaykh's behavior—be it angry, scolding, smiling, or weeping—has a purpose behind it.

A story is sometimes told to illustrate this point. (Taken out of context, this story may be misinterpreted, but as it conveys an important lesson related to your question, I will tell it.) Once a teacher privately asked his wife to slip out of their house, disguise herself, and then return home. Obviously, any student who saw her entering the house in disguise would be likely to suspect that she was not the shaykh's wife, but some other woman. She did as her husband had asked: slipped out when no one was looking, dressed in borrowed clothes, and then—choosing a moment when all the students were watching—returned to the private quarters of the house. She stayed inside for some time. The students grew suspicious. Hours passed, and she had not emerged. Finally, all the students but one stood up and left, thinking ill of the shaykh.

The teacher emerged from his home and saw the single student who remained. He asked, "Why didn't you leave?" The student replied, "I am not concerned with your private affairs. I have come to learn what you have to teach." The teacher embraced the student, praising his attitude and explaining that the woman was his wife.

All of the teacher's acts are meaningful, including those that appear to test the student. The aspirant will not discern or benefit from their meaning if he or she does not trust the teacher. There can be no place for distrust, misunderstanding, or doubt in the relationship with the guide.

In one particular *khānaqāh* (Sufi study center), many students lived and practiced for a long time. A newcomer arrived, quickly made progress, and was taken as a *khalīfah* (deputy) by the shaykh. The senior students were distressed and filled with misgivings, for they had worked long and hard, yet this newcomer was being favored above them. Noticing their discontent, the teacher said, "I am willing, wishing, and praying for improvement in all of you. If you make progress like our new friend, I will make you all deputies. Right now, however, you are like freshly hewn logs that are still green. Although I give all my warmth to these logs, they don't catch fire. The new student is a well-seasoned piece of wood. With a little effort, he has made great progress." Then the students understood.

In short, one should not be suspicious of one's shaykh. Always assume that there is a good reason for the teacher's actions. If one becomes possessed by doubts or distrust, then it is best to meet privately, express one's confusion, and resolve the matter.

***

Question 30: Academic Study of Sufism

Can the academic study of Sufism assist journeyers on the path? Is it recommended that students read works by famous Sufi masters and scholars of Islam?

Reading the works of shaykhs and scholars may clarify some subjects. However, if a student of Sufism inclines toward or is assigned readings, his or her primary goal should be to raise questions to bring to the study of the Qur'ān and to discussions with the shaykh. Simply accumulating intellectual knowledge serves little purpose for the seeker.

No matter how many books a person reads about Sufism, he or she will not gain its essence, for it is not a solely academic discipline. *Taṣawwuf* is a journey that takes place within us, changing the totality of our being. *Sāliks* (spiritual travelers) undertake a concrete program of training. They do not speculate on cosmic principles and heightened states of being, philosophical issues or creeds. They work. They do practices that refine intuitive perception, and in so doing, come to understand the principles of Sufism for themselves. The Persian shaykh Abū al-Qāsim al-Qushayrī (r.a.) (d. 1072) wrote, "'The learned man imitates examples,' it is said, 'but the gnostic receives living guidance.'"[50]

Do you think that by reading volumes on Sufism, seekers can achieve the goal? No, no, those who yearn to know the truth should throw away their books and meditate.

If someone says, "Tell me about Sufism,"
what is the best way to answer, if not by
means of intellectual explanations?

If someone asks about Sufism, you can say that on the one hand, there is the history and scholarship of Sufism, and on the other hand, there is the reality of being a Sufi. Sufism is like swimming. If you read books on swimming, you will not be able to swim. Conversely, talented swimmers are known for their grace and speed in the water, not for their commentaries on technique.

To communicate Sufism to others, focus on your meditation, for meditation will bring about changes in you that will affect those around you far more than words ever could. Do the practices; then wherever you are, the people you meet will be affected by the light that you carry in your heart.

The Caliph 'Umar ؓ (d. 644), who was appointed leader of the Muslim community in 634 C.E., usually wore common, threadbare garments, many of them mended with patches. Once when a foreign delegation was on its way to meet with him in Medina, his associates wondered aloud whether he might change into something more befitting a head of state. He replied, "Do you think it is my outer garb that will impress these ambassadors? They have better clothing than I. But if I have something in my heart, then God willing, they will sense and respond to that."

Throughout the delegates' visit, the caliph wore his usual attire. Despite his humble appearance, the guests departed deeply moved.

Others will be touched by that which is within you, not that which you put on to fit their expectations. Whatever your job—practicing a trade, looking after your family, teaching, doing clerical work, running a business, serving others—even though your responsibilities may seem unrelated to Sufism, those around you will be affected by your inner qualities. Perhaps they will feel peaceful, uplifted, or more contented in your presence. They may sense that there is something unique about you. If they then say, "Did I hear you mention Sufism? I'd like to know more about that," you can reply, "Why not join me in meditation? That's the best way to start to understand."

***

Question 31: Centers of Consciousness (*Laṭā'if*)

You have referred to the "laṭā'if," defining them as "centers of consciousness." Would you please describe these centers in more detail? Are they the same as the chakras in yoga, or related to the psychological terms "id," "ego," and "superego"? What is their significance?

It is generally thought that the human body contains only one center of consciousness: the mind or brain. But the elder Sufis, through their spiritual experiences, discovered additional centers of perception or inner senses which they referred to as *laṭā'if* (singular: *laṭīfah*). They further concluded based on their *kashf* (intuitive insight) that there are ten such *laṭā'if*.

The origins of the *laṭā'if* reflect the origins of the universe as a whole. According to Shaykh Aḥmad Farūqī Sirhindī (r.a.) (d. 1624), the Indian master from whom the Mujadiddi lineage descends, God created the universe in two stages. First came *'ālam al-amr* (the world of God's command), which emerged instantly when God said, "Be!" Then God created *'ālam al-khalq* (the world of creation) through a process of evolution that lasted many years. After *'ālam al-khalq*, God created the human being. God blessed this new creation with certain inner faculties or points of light: the *laṭā'if*. Five of the *laṭā'if*—*nafs* (self), *bād* (air), nār (fire), *mā'* (water), and *khāk* (earth)—were part of the world of creation. The other five—*qalb* (heart), *rūḥ* (spirit), *sirr* (secret), *khafī* (hidden), and *akhfā* (most hidden)—were part of the world of God's command.

The *laṭā'if* were luminous initially. When God connected them to the body, their light started to be filtered through the influences of the physical world, including human beings' tendency to identify with materiality. The dimming of our natural inner radiance is reflected in the Qur'ānic passage, *Surely We created the human being of the best stature, then We reduced him to the lowest of the low....*[51] Through practices that involve concentrating on the *laṭā'if*, the Sufi aspirant becomes able to use them as means to greater awareness of the Divine Presence. The more the seeker develops this ability, the less the light of knowledge is obscured.

Like the faculty of memory, the *laṭā'if* are faculties that we may sense and experience, yet have difficulty explaining. How would you define memory? You might say it resides in the brain—you might even describe its physiological workings—but these descriptions fail to convey all its dimensions. Sometimes, a person loses his or her memory due to injury. He or she becomes even more aware of its importance, yet is no better able to explain it. Similarly, the *laṭā'if* cannot be adequately defined in words; but as a person brings them to light, he or she comes to understand them.

Different Sufi orders have associated the *laṭā'if* with various locations on the body. The Naqshbandī-Mujaddidī Order places the five centers of the world of God's command (the *laṭā'if* of *'ālam al-amr*) in the chest. The heart or *qalb* is on the left side of the body, two inches below the nipple. The spirit, *rūḥ*, is in the corresponding position on the right side of the chest. The center known as "secret," or *sirr*, is on the same side as the heart, but above the breast. "Hidden" (*khafī*) is on the right above the breast. "Most hidden" (*akhfā*) is in the middle of the chest, between the heart and spirit.

Shaykhs of the Naqshbandī-Mujaddidī Order guide the *sālik* (spiritual traveler) in enlightening the *laṭā'if* one by one. This is accomplished primarily through *murāqabah* (meditation). While sitting, the student makes an intention (*niyāh*) to pay attention to a particular center. He or she focuses first on the heart (*qalb*), then, in sequence, the other *laṭā'if* of the world of God's command: spirit, secret, hidden, and most hidden (*rūḥ*, *sirr*, *khafī*, and *akhfā*). When these are fully enlightened, the student pays attention to the *laṭā'if* associated with the world of creation (*'ālam al-khalq*).

Of the centers connected with the world of creation, only the self or *nafs* is regarded as corresponding to a particular point on the human body. Its location is in the middle of the forehead. It is the first of the *laṭā'if* of *'ālam al-khalq* that the student refines, for it is considered the sum total of all the others. After concentrating on the self for some time, the student is guided next to focus on the four elements of which the body is constituted—air, fire, water, and earth (*bād*, nār, *mā'*, and *khāk*). When these are infused with light, every pore of the body becomes illuminated and starts to remember God. This total engagement in remembrance is called *sulṭān al-adhkār*: the remembrance par excellence.[52]

While shaykhs of many orders have had knowledge of the *laṭā'if,* the methods that Naqshbandī-Mujaddidī teachers use to refine them are distinctive in several ways. First, Bahā'uddīn Naqshband (r.a.) (d. 1389), the Central Asian shaykh from whom the order takes its name, re-formulated the sequence in which the *laṭā'if* were illumined. Other orders dealt with the *laṭā'if* of the world of creation before refining those of the world of command. Bahā'uddīn Naqshband (r.a.) altered the sequence so that students began with the heart (*qalb*), then proceeded through the other *laṭā'if* of the world of God's command, and only then turned to the self (*nafs*) and other *laṭā'if* of the world of creation. This approach became known as *indiraj an-nihayah fi'l-bidayah* ("where others end, there marks our beginning").[53]

Roughly two centuries later, Shaykh Aḥmad Farūqī Sirhindī (r.a.) further developed the Naqshbandī-Mujaddidī techniques for enlightening the *laṭā'if*. Based on his own findings, he identified ten *laṭā'if* and formulated a series of intentions or *niyāhs* through which seekers could progressively refine these in meditation. Earlier shaykhs had described the path in terms of stations and states,[54] or in terms of degrees of love for the shaykh, the Prophet ﷺ, and God. Within their formulations, it remained a mystery how, when, and to what level a student might progress. In contrast, Shaykh Aḥmad Farūqī Sirhindī (r.a.) organized the teachings in such a way as to provide a curriculum for spiritual training.

The *awliyā'* (saints) have observed certain colors when concentrating on the *laṭā'if*. The color or light associated with *qalb* (heart) is golden. *Rūḥ* (spirit) has been perceived as red with a hint of gold. *Sirr* (secret) is identified with pure white; *khafī* (hidden) with black; *akhfā* (most hidden) with green; and *nafs* (self) with the azure blue of the fall sky. These colors were identified through the experiences of the elders, who reported whichever colors they saw in meditation. Naturally, their observations sometimes differed. However, when one elder said that the heart appeared golden to him, and others said the same, then the blessing and light of the heart were understood to be golden. The colors of the other *laṭā'if* were established in the same way.

Because these delineations were merely matters of intuitive insight, it is not necessary for every seeker to see the same color; nor is seeing color the objective. If a person sees colors, well and good. If a person does not, that is fine, too. The object is to remember God, not to have visions.

From a Sufi point of view, spiritual guidance depends on the prophets. The Divine revelation and *sharī'ah* (religious or sacred law) came to humanity through the prophets alone, and only the paths which they have trod are straight and correct. These paths are reflected in the *laṭā'if* of the world of God's command, each of which was adopted by a prophet as the means through which to attain nearness to God. *Qalb* (heart) is said to be under the feet of Adam عليه السلام. *Rūḥ* (spirit) is under the feet of Abraham عليه السلام, while *sirr* (secret) is under the feet of Moses عليه السلام. *Khafī* (hidden) is under the feet of Jesus Christ عليه السلام, and *akhfā* (most hidden) is under the feet of the Prophet Muhammad ﷺ.

This explanation should make clear the vast difference between the *laṭā'if* and the *chakras* that are described by yogis. I think you can also see that psychological terms like "id," "ego," and "superego" have no connection to the *laṭā'if*.

To address your question regarding the significance of the *laṭā'if*, let me share a passage by Shāh Walīullāh (r.a.) (d. 1762), a leading eighteenth-century theologian of Delhi. About a century after Shaykh Aḥmad Farūqī Sirhindī (r.a.) gave his comprehensive account of the *laṭā'if*, Shāh Walīullāh (r.a.) reflected:

> In endowing them with the knowledge of the higher functions [*laṭā'if*], God has given later Sufis an invaluable balancing factor. The better one is acquainted with such faculties, the better one is able to refine them; and

whoever is ablest in discerning their various characteristics is also the ablest guide for seekers of that knowledge.

To illustrate the difference between someone who possesses the knowledge of these faculties and those people who...[have not] gained any of this knowledge, we might compare the former to a physician, skilled in the diagnosis of various types of illnesses, who knows their causes, their symptoms, the methods of treatment, and all the rules which the ancients evolved after long, protracted experience. To continue the analogy, someone who lacks such knowledge is like an unqualified physician....

Briefly, then, if you wish to know the path taken by those who have reached the stage of establishment and have become heirs to the prophetic endowment, it is important that you should realize that this is not possible without a knowledge of these faculties... [This] knowledge...is an immense blessing which has been bestowed upon recent times. *It is the bounty of God, bestowed upon us and upon humanity—yet most people are not grateful.*[55]

***

Question 32: "Where Others End, There Marks Our Beginning" (*Indiraj an-nihayah fi'l-bidayah*)

Would you please elaborate on the concept of "indiraj an-nihayah fi'l-bidayah"?

Indirāj an-nihāyah fi'l-bidāyah, meaning "where others end, there marks our beginning," is used in the Naqshbandī-Mujaddidī Order to describe a distinctive sequencing of spiritual practices. Introduced by Shaykh Bahā'uddīn Naqshband in the fourteenth century, it is a technique designed to aid in overcoming the obstacles that keep human beings from drawing near to God.

Two kinds of distractions interfere with our awareness of the Creator. First are distractions of the external world that attract our interest, occupy our attention, and cause us to forget God. Such distractions are related to the self (*nafs*). Second are distractions that come from within us and are associated with the heart (*qalb*). To draw nearer to God, we must become free of both outer and inner obstacles.

Early shaykhs often directed the initial stages of spiritual training toward overcoming the distractions of the outer world and *nafs*. They guided students first to refine the centers of consciousness associated with the world of creation (the *laṭā'if* of *'ālam al-khalq*). The technical term for this undertaking is "the journey to the horizon" (*sayr-i āfāqī*). Only when *sayr-i āfāqī* was completed would students perfect the centers that relate most directly to one's interior life: the heart and the other *laṭā'if* of *'ālam al-amr*. This aspect of the path is called "the journey toward inner being" (*sayr-i anfusī*).

Conquering the self was a difficult undertaking, and novices could commit many errors in the attempt. Those who started with this step often spent years refining themselves through austerities. The approach proved so time-consuming that spiritual travelers frequently died before reaching their destination.

Noting the hardships that this approach could entail, Bahā'uddīn Naqshband (r.a.) (d. 1389) altered the practices taught by his predecessors. He guided his students to begin the process of transformation with the heart rather than the self. This technique became known within the Naqshbandi Order as *indirāj an-nihāyah fi'l-bidāyah*—"where others end, there marks our beginning."

Bahā'uddīn Naqshband (r.a.) and his successors found that students trained in this technique often reached their spiritual destination more quickly. After completing "the journey toward the inner being," they did not need to devote extra time to completing "the journey to the horizon," for in the process of pursuing the former they were simultaneously advancing in the latter.

Some people wonder: if they start their journey where others end, then what is the end of their journey? "Where others end, there marks our beginning" does not mean that novices who use this technique will, from the outset, attain the excellence and perfection that earlier saints attained at the end. They receive only a taste of the final destination at the beginning. Bahā'uddīn Naqshband (r.a.) hoped that this taste would arouse students' yearning and courage to walk the spiritual path. The experience of the eternal truth in its fullness marks the last stage of the path, an experience which Bahā'uddīn Naqshband (r.a.) said is to stand spellbound and become mute.

One day a visitor asked Khwājah Bahā'uddīn Naqshband (r.a.), "What is the secret which enables a seeker in your order to be so affected and gain so much insight in the initial stages of study?"

He replied, "In contrast to seekers of the past, today's students are subject to constant distractions that diminish their yearning, intention, and will power. Nevertheless, the love we feel toward them has compelled us to find a way to deal with their need. So, with the help of the Almighty, we have devised an appropriate method. Whether or not seekers have made any significant effort, we provide them at the beginning with a glimpse of their ultimate goal. Having once sensed the fulfillment that lies ahead, even the most cold and unresponsive hearts become warm and receptive."

***

Question 33: Transmission (*Tawajjuh*) and Affinity (*Nisbah*)

You have said that in your particular order, training takes place through "tawajjuh" (transmission) and "nisbah" (affinity between the student and the guide). How did these aspects of Sufism develop, and why are they used? Were they introduced by the Prophet Muhammad ﷺ?

Tawajjuh (transmission[56]) and *nisbah* (affinity between the student and the guide) are facets of the process through which the shaykh, by virtue of his or her inner state, seeks to uplift the student's state. The light transmitted to the shaykh's heart by his or her own teacher is transmitted in turn to the seeker's heart. As the student continues to make effort in the practices, this spark one day becomes a flame.

A precedent for *tawajjuh* may be found in the story of the angel Gabriel ؑ imparting the first verses of the Qur'ān to the Prophet Muhammad ﷺ. Gabriel ؑ appeared to the

Prophet ﷺ and commanded, “Read!” The Prophet ﷺ, who was illiterate, replied, “I cannot read.” Gabriel ﵇ embraced the Prophet ﷺ, then commanded again, “Read!” The Prophet ﷺ repeated, “I cannot.” A second time Gabriel ﵇ pressed the Prophet ﷺ to him, declaring, “Read!” The Prophet ﷺ replied, “I cannot.” For the third time, Gabriel ﵇ seized the Prophet ﷺ; and in that embrace, the Prophet ﷺ gained the ability to “read,” to receive and understand God’s message to humanity.[57] According to Islamic scholars, Ḥazrat Gabriel ﵇ conveyed this capacity and knowledge from the unseen by means of *tawajjuh*.

An exchange between the Prophet Muhammad ﷺ and his companion ‘Umar ibn al-Khaṭṭāb[58] ﵁ demonstrates *tawajjuh* in conjunction with *nisbah*, a relationship of personal affinity, congeniality, and attachment. The Holy Prophet ﷺ said, “One is not a perfect Muslim if one does not love Allah and Allah’s Prophet more than one loves one’s self, one’s wealth, one’s children, and all other people.” ‘Umar ﵁ replied, “My love is indeed not so.” There was a short silence between them. Then ‘Umar ﵁ confessed, “I do not find my love for Allah and the Prophet ﷺ surmounting my love for myself.” There was another silence; then ‘Umar ﵁ exclaimed, “My love for Allah and the Prophet ﷺ is now greater than my love for everything else!”

These two stories show progressive realizations emerging from a series of transmissions that are fostered by inner attunement. Similarly, the unique relationship between the seeker and the shaykh (*nisbah*) enables the training through *tawajjuh* to take place.

We must remember that whoever gives transmission is not the source of change or inspiration. The originator is God, without Whose blessings no change can occur. The attainment of human beings’ highest destiny cannot be accomplished through any person, being, or system but only through the agency of the Almighty. However, the right path has been demonstrated by the prophets of God and their chosen representatives throughout the generations by means of speech, action, accompaniment, and transmission.

Methods of teaching vary. Some *ṭarīqahs* (orders) use advice and sermons, and others focus on service; some stress *dhikr* (remembrance) and *du'ā'* (supplication), while others celebrate the anniversaries[59] of Sufi masters, and yet others listen to poetry or *qawwālī* (devotional music). Shaykhs of the Naqshbandī-Mujaddidī Order use tried and tested methods based on *nisbah* and *tawajjuh*, coupled with firm adherence to the *sunnah* (example and teachings of the Prophet Muhammad ﷺ).

Critics claim that some Sufi practices are improper innovations (*bid'a*), pointing out that they were not performed during the time of the Prophet Muhammad ﷺ, his companions, or the companions' followers. While it is true that not all these methods were used during the Prophet's lifetime, the essence of Sufism has always been present. The accompaniment of the Holy Prophet ﷺ had a profound effect, for he could provide knowledge and wisdom of every kind. One glance from the Prophet ﷺ could take a believer through all the stages of realization. This power and spiritual intensity gave his companions an advantage that later generations did not enjoy. Those who heard him grasped the beliefs he explained immediately. If questions arose, the companions could ask the Prophet ﷺ for decisions and dispensations then and there.

God imparted to the Holy Prophet ﷺ the basic tenets of the law in all its aspects, and these the Prophet ﷺ passed on to his community. But many specific regulations and exact details were not formalized until after his death. During his lifetime, no books on jurisprudence were written; no complex rules for interpreting his statements and actions were developed; the arguments of faith were not enumerated in texts. The passage of time and the requirements of different circumstances gradually led to the compilation of Islamic knowledge. Later generations considered it important to frame regulations and to preserve and codify the expressions of the Prophet ﷺ. Scholars and theologians published volumes on many aspects of Islam as they strove to refine their disciplines.

While some Muslims focused on elucidating such topics as Islamic economics, criminal law, technicalities of *ṣalāh* (prayer), and so on, those who pursued the spiritual path focused on remembrance of God. They aspired toward not only periodic remembrance, but constant remembrance. To this end, they developed techniques for awakening the heart, adapting them to suit the prevailing circumstances. Today the teachings available within the different orders bear witness to the noble efforts made by many great souls as they sought God's nearness and friendship.

These efforts conformed fully with the example and sayings of the Holy Prophet ﷺ. In return, the Almighty rewarded the tribulations of the Sufi masters with acceptance. No one can criticize or demean such *awliyā'* (saints) as Shaykh 'Abd al-Qādir Jīlānī of Baghdad (r.a.) (d. 1077), founder of the Qādirī Order; Khwājah Moinuddīn Chishtī (r.a.) (d. 1236), who spread the teachings of the Chishtī Order in India; Ḥazrat Abū al-Ḥasan Shādhilī (r.a.) (d. 1258), the North African shaykh and founder of the Shādhilī Order; Khwājah Bahā'uddīn Naqshband of Bukhara (r.a.) (d. 1389), from whom the Naqshbandī lineage descends; Indian Muslim reformer Shaykh Aḥmad Farūqī

Sirhindī (r.a.) (d. 1624), founder of the Mujaddidī lineage; and the many saintly souls who lived before and after them—for all were people of piety, deep understanding, perseverance, submission, and upright character.

***

Question 34: Meditation (*Murāqabah*)

I understand that students of your particular branch of the Naqshbandī-Mujaddidī Order devote much effort to "murāqabah," or meditation. Would you kindly explain this practice?

Experience over the centuries has shown that *murāqabah* leads to all stages of perfection. For this reason, although shaykhs of our order also perform *dhikr* (recitations evoking remembrance of God), *durūd* (supplications for blessings upon the Prophet ﷺ), and recitations, *murāqabah* is the most important component of their inner work.

The origin of *murāqabah* lies in the saying of the Prophet Muhammad ﷺ, "Adore Allah as if you are seeing Him, and if you do not see Him, know that He is seeing you."[60] Literally, *murāqabah* means to wait and to guarantee or protect. When used as a Sufi technical term, its meaning varies among orders. The Naqshbandī-Mujaddidī *ṭarīqah* defines *murāqabah* most simply as sitting with one's eyes closed and waiting for blessings from the Holy Essence (the Source of all blessings and bounties). It is the art of withdrawing from the external stimuli of the world and redirecting one's attention toward God via the transmissions and *niyāhs* (intentions) received from one's shaykh.

Traditionally, students of many orders renounced the world for decades, if not for their entire lives. The techniques formulated by Shaykh Aḥmad Farūqī Sirhindī (r.a.) made such prolonged renunciation unnecessary. In the nineteenth century, another Indian master, Sayyid 'Abd al-Bāri Shah (r.a.) (d. 1900), further adapted the teachings to be even more accessible to *sāliks* (spiritual travelers) and better suited to conditions in the modern world. The resulting approach is fully compatible with today's lifestyles, but it is also very delicate. This is why we sit in *murāqabah*. Without austerities, without prolonged seclusion, we emphasize *murāqabah* as the way to refine the *laṭā'if*, our receivers for the blessings of God.

Sitting in *murāqabah* is a form of renunciation, but it is renunciation several times daily for forty minutes, not continually for twenty or more years. One is asked to turn away from the world for that period of time, to pay attention to something else. For forty minutes, one turns one's back on daily affairs. One entrusts all matters to God, and God takes care of everything.

The Central Asian master Sa'duddīn Kāshgharī (r.a.) (d. 860) once heard Shaykh Junayd of Baghdad (r.a.) (d. 910) say, "A cat taught me *murāqabah*. One day I saw her sitting near the hole of a mouse. She sat so attentively, not a pore of her body moved. I was watching her with great astonishment when suddenly, I heard a voice say, 'O idle one, I am no less your aim and object than a mouse is the object of the cat. You should strive toward Me no less than the cat strives toward its prey!'"

Silence is the knock upon the inner door. If one were expecting visitors, one would not turn on an electric drill or vacuum cleaner, knowing its noise would drown out the doorbell. Similarly, the student of Sufism approaches *murāqabah* with an attitude of silence and concentration.

Murāqabah has been described as "the flow of consciousness to the Divine." It is conscious involvement, not unconscious relaxation. It is being aware of the qualities that are being activated inwardly in the moment. Another definition of *murāqabah* is vigilance. Vigilance means attentiveness: a vigil is a period of time during which one remains attentive.

When engaging in *murāqabah*, the student expresses his or her will to be attentive through intention. In daily life, intention precedes purposeful action or thought that is undertaken by deliberate decision. In the context of Sufi meditation, intention or *niyāh* is the technical term for a statement recited silently each time one sits in order to direct the mind and heart toward the object of desire: God. The shaykh assigns *niyāhs* to the student in a specific progression. Each *niyāh* refines a particular *laṭīfah* (subtle center of perception), so that through that center, the student may become more attuned to the transmissions coming from other dimensions.

Some mystical schools regard quieting the mind as the ultimate attainment. When one is able to empty the mind of thoughts, worries subside; one feels at peace. Equating this sense of peace with spiritual realization, many techniques focus on controlling the thoughts.

The focus of the seeker engaged in Sufi practices lies elsewhere. He or she leaves the mind alone, letting it do its work, while he or she proceeds with awakening the *laṭā'if.* In *murāqabah*, thoughts pass through the mind, coming and going, wandering here and there. The disciple of Sufism does not try to follow them. Have you ever sat in a restaurant or a bus stop, just watching and letting whatever passes before your vision come and go? Such is the detachment of *murāqabah*. After some time, thoughts quiet down, and one becomes unaware of one's being. One is lost in meditation. In that state, one drifts from this dimension to another, as a boat drifts on a current beyond its control yet carrying it towards the destination. One gains new insights and deeper understandings of God, the universe, and one's fellow human beings. One may also feel some activity in the *laṭā'if*, in one's chest. A sense of interest or attraction arises, drawing one to spend more time in *murāqabah* and furthering progress on the path.

Little by little, the practice of *murāqabah* reconditions the entire being. The *sālik* ultimately may undergo progressive transformations until he or she comes to the final stages of *fanā'* (annihilation) and *baqā'* (subsistence), when not only the *laṭā'if* but the whole body becomes enlightened. The Holy Prophet ﷺ used to pray, "O Allah, let there be light in front of me. Let there be light behind me. Let there be light above me and below me and to my left and to my right, and make light a part of me..."

Murāqabah implies voluntarily opening oneself to transformation. Many people approach meditation with attitudes akin to "Let's see what I can get from this" or with hopes of gaining psychic or supernatural powers. In *murāqabah,* those who follow the Sufi path strive to be nothing other than what they most truly are. They observe with a willingness to see and hear, not with a desire for phenomena (although phenomena may transpire). There is nothing more phenomenal than one's own transformation. To become saintly is the greatest phenomenon. The power of compassion, peace, and love is the greatest power.

In the silence of *murāqabah*, all the distractions, disturbances, inner dialogues, doubts, fears, and contradictions of the mind become still. In the tranquillity of meditation, as on a quiet pond, the slightest breeze creates a ripple. When one has ceased disturbing the pond, the gentle breezes of knowledge and reality can be detected through their action upon the inner self. One becomes open to receiving blessings in abundance, and able to understand the significance of worlds beyond this world.

***

Question 35: Awakening the Heart

What does it mean for the heart to become "awakened" or "enlightened"?

As we have discussed, human beings have inner centers of consciousness, or *laṭā'if*. Of the ten *laṭā'if* recognized by the Naqshbandī-Mujaddidī Order, *laṭīfah qalb* (heart) has special importance. An-Nu'mān ibn Bashīr 🙶 narrated that the Prophet Muhammad 🙵 said, "There is a piece of flesh in the body such that if it is reformed, the whole body becomes good, and if it spoils, the whole body becomes spoiled. That [piece of flesh] is the heart."

With the help of the practices, transmissions, and the shaykh's attention, even in the early phases of study the *sālik* (spiritual traveler) feels effects in his or her heart. Some students experience a sensation like the ticking of a clock; others detect something like the singing of sparrows or water bubbling in a teapot. The renowned Persian Sufi poet Ḥāfiẓ (r.a.) (d. 1391) hints at the heart's movement in a couplet:

No one knows the destination of the beloved.
No one knows where stands the mansion of
the beloved. [One knows] only this: that the
sound of a ringing bell is approaching.

Another poet wrote, "The pounding heart tells me that the beloved has passed this way."

As the *sālik* devotes more time to *murāqabah* (meditation), the heart continues to be polished until it becomes like a mirror, accurately reflecting events and circumstances around it. The heart is "open" when the remembrance of God engages it fully. Light suffuses the heart, revealing aspects of reality that previously lay hidden. There dawns a new, more complete understanding of life in all its aspects. In short, the seeker is enlightened.

The Indian master Sayyid 'Abd al-Bāri Shah (r.a.) (d. 1900) once said, "To restore life to a dead person is not a miracle." His student Ḥazrat Ḥāmid Ḥasan 'Alawī (r.a.) (d. 1959) asked in amazement, "If reviving the dead does not constitute a miracle, what does?" Sayyid 'Abd al-Bāri Shah (r.a.) replied, "The greater task is to awaken a lifeless heart. To awaken a dead heart is not within the reach of any person unless and until the grace of God supports this effort."

As I have mentioned, in accordance with the principle of *indiraj an-nihayah fi'l-bidayah* ("where others end, there marks our beginning"), students of our particular order start by concentrating on the heart. From the time a student receives the first transmission, his or her *qalb* is being gradually awakened.

The tongue may tire of repeating *dhikr* (recitations invoking the Presence of God) for any length of time. But the awakened heart busies itself in recollecting the Almighty every moment. This constant remembrance of God in the heart is called *dhikr al-qalb*. Step by step, veils of darkness give way to light, understanding, and insight. The seeker beholds dimensions which the five senses could never detect nor the mind imagine. The Prophet Muhammad ﷺ said, "Beware of the deep understanding of a believer, for the believer perceives with the aid of the Light of Allah."

***

Question 36: Remembrance (*Dhikr*)

Would you please expand upon the meaning of the term "dhikr"? How is "dhikr" done? What is its importance to the student?

Sufi masters stress *dhikr* (remembrance), for it grounds the belief, knowledge, and faith of the seeker by focusing his or her attention on God.

One of the fundamental commands of God is to do *dhikr* as often as possible until continual awareness of the Divine Presence is established. God revealed to Moses ﷷ, *Verily, I—I alone—am God; there is no deity save Me. Hence worship Me alone and be constant in prayer so as to remember Me!*[61] This command for *dhikr* has extended to all generations, although the forms of *dhikr* have varied with time and place.

The companions of the Prophet Muhammad ﷺ did not perform *dhikr* as a formal technique, for one look from the Prophet ﷺ could elevate a person's consciousness. When Islamic teachings were compiled after the Prophet's death, individuals who sought a state of remembrance similar to that achieved by the companions found in *dhikr* a critical means. They designated *dhikr* a core practice of Sufism and set about identifying the most effective ways to perform it.

One *dhikr* popular among early Sufi masters and still widely used is saying *lā ilāha illāllāh* (there is no god but God). The negative "no god" is followed by the affirmative "but God," with force exerted on the latter. Another form of *dhikr* is to repeat *Allah* (the proper name of God) when given permission by one's spiritual mentor to do so. These phrases are recited in specific ways to facilitate remembrance. Some orders do *dhikr* while standing, some while sitting in a certain posture, and some while moving. Shaykhs introduced these variations to intensify the *dhikr*.

Dhikr may be recited *jalī* (aloud) or *khafī* (silently in the heart). Some orders stress the former, while others emphasize the latter. Both types of *dhikr* offer the same benefits. They differ only in technique. Both forms also find justification in guidance given by the Prophet Muhammad ﷺ. Muhammad Mahmood Ali Qutbi notes that "the advocates of the *jalī* rely on the Tradition of the Prophet ﷺ, 'Remember God to such an extent that people call you mad.' *Khafī* (silent) is [based] upon the Tradition, 'You are not addressing a deaf and an absent being, but you call unto a Being who is hearing you, seeing you, and is present with you wherever you are.'"[62] Ḥazrat 'Ā'ishah ؓ, wife of the Prophet ﷺ, reported that he said:

> *Dhikr khafī*, which is not heard by angels, is rewarded seventy times over. When, on the Day of Resurrection, Allah will summon all the creation for reckoning, the recording angels will bring the recorded accounts of all the people, and Allah will ask them to verify if there are any more good deeds to the credit of a certain individual. They will submit that they have not omitted anything from his or her recorded account. Allah will then say, "There is yet one good deed to this person's credit, which is not known to the angels: doing *dhikr* in silence."[63]

Given that both types of *dhikr* are commended by the Prophet ﷺ, Shaikhul Ḥadīth Maulana Muhammad Zakariyya concludes that "either form of *dhikr* is important under different sets of conditions. It is for the shaykh of a person to prescribe the best form of *dhikr* for him [or her] at a particular time."[64]

Shaykhs of the Naqshbandī line until the time of the Central Asian master Khwājah Amīr Kulāl Sūkhārī (r.a.) (d. 1370) performed *dhikr* both *jalī* and *khafī*. Khwājah Amīr Kulāl's student, Bahā'uddīn Naqshband (r.a.) (d. 1389), was instructed by an earlier shaykh of the order, 'Abd al-Khāliq Ghujduwānī (r.a.) (d. 1179),[65] to avoid *dhikr jalī* and always do *dhikr khafī*. From that time, silent remembrance has been an essential feature of the Naqshbandī-Mujaddidī Order.

Nevertheless, shaykhs of this order also may prescribe *dhikr* to be done aloud. For example, the teacher may assign *dhikr jalī* to a seeker who seems unreceptive to the effects of other practices. Students who do this form of *dhikr* often experience a pleasant sensation of warmth inside the body. Finding the recitations rewarding, they are inspired to carry on with the practices. Shaykhs may also assign *dhikr jalī* to students who have difficulty focusing, for vocal repetitions can overpower the thoughts and quiet the mind.

Whether through *dhikr* said aloud or silently, those who strive in the way of Sufism aspire to remember God in every condition. The Qur'ān states, *They remember Allah standing, sitting, and on their sides.*[66] Once my shaykh asked his teacher to explain *dhikr kathīr* (remembering [God] much), a practice enjoined in the Qur'ān.[67] My shaykh expected instructions regarding the number of recitations to be done. Instead, his guide replied that "remembering God much" is not a matter of quantity: it is a matter of forgetting everything other than God.

One day, the Indian master Sayyid 'Abd al-Bāri Shah (r.a.) (d. 1900) was performing *dhikr* according to the methods of the Chishtī Order. Suddenly, Ḥazrat Moinuddīn Chishtī himself (r.a.) (d. 1236) appeared to him in a vision. Taking him to the side of a mountain, Moinuddīn Chishtī (r.a.) showed him a devotee who was reciting the *dhikr an-nafi wa'l-ithbāt* (negation and affirmation) aloud. When this man uttered *lā ilāha*, the mountain seemed to fall into two pieces; when he said *illāllāh*, the mountain returned to its previous state. They stood some time watching the devotee doing recitations. At length, Moinuddīn Chishtī (r.a.) said, "This is the way to perform *dhikr*."

Through *dhikr,* Sufi masters train students to purify their hearts and souls. The shaykh's role is to guide seekers to the original remembrance: to enable them to become continuously and spontaneously aware of the Divine Presence in the physical, mental, and emotional aspects of life, in the outer and inner realms.

The student should carefully follow the shaykh's instructions regarding the manner in which *dhikr* is to be performed. To illustrate this point, the story is told of a student who lived with his family on a farm, far away from his shaykh. Periodically, he would make the long journey to visit his guide and receive instruction. During one such visit, he asked the shaykh for recitations to perform. The shaykh advised him to recite *lā ilāha illāllāh* five hundred times daily.

The disciple returned home. Each day, he faithfully recited the *dhikr* five hundred times. After some months, it occurred to him that perhaps he should increase the number. He started doing two thousand a day. A little later, he increased the number to five thousand, then to seven thousand, until finally he was doing ten thousand recitations daily.

Gradually, the animals on the farm began to die. When they were all dead, the man's children and wife left him. In the end, he lost everything.

Distraught, the disciple went back to the shaykh and told him what had happened. The shaykh asked, "How many *dhikr* are you doing?" "Ten thousand," the student replied. The shaykh was astounded and upset. To recite *lā ilāha illāllāh* is to affirm that nothing exists but God. The student had taken to negating everything but God with such fervor that everything but God was being removed from his life.

The shaykh directed the student to recite a certain *durūd* (a prayer asking for the blessings of God upon the Prophet Muhammad ﷺ). The student returned home and did the prayer as directed. Soon his wife and children returned, his farm began to prosper again, and his life resumed its normal course.

Usually, the formal recitations of *dhikr* are repeated one thousand, two thousand, or at most five thousand times once a day. The student must not increase the number without the permission of the shaykh. Whenever one makes such an increase, one should be willing to commit to doing that number of recitations regularly until one's last breath. Anything that is recited must be recited daily. Ḥazrat 'Abd al-Bāri Shah (r.a.) would sit in the mosque each day to do his practices, and every time he took on a new recitation, he would never miss performing it from that time forward. While relatively few recitations are assigned, those that are assigned must be completed regularly.

To remember God throughout day-to-day life is far more valuable than periodically making a show of remembrance. *Dhikr* is not a ceremony. It is the very object of life. The person who remembers God finds happiness; the person who forgets finds only desolation. Forgetfulness is the petrifying force that turns a tree to stone. In contrast, through *dhikr*, the aspirant achieves the mercy of God and the angels, purity of spirit, and adornment of the soul. Progress becomes easy, and the seeker draws near to the Almighty, for God has said, *Remember Me and I shall remember you.*[68]

***

Question 37: Finding Time for Self-Refinement

I think many people have trouble finding time for spiritual practices. If students of Sufism cannot devote time to meditation, are there other ways they can refine themselves in the course of their daily lives?

The practices refine intuition, and intuition is a key to bringing forth higher qualities. Shaykhs of our particular order seldom use speech or verbal instructions to direct students in improving their characters. Students are expected, with the help of the practices, to intuitively become aware of their shortcomings and then strive to overcome them. This is a classical route to perfection. But as you seem keen on receiving oral instruction in this regard, let me suggest the following.

As you know, students of most Sufi orders today do not renounce the world, but rather take part in family and professional life while also performing practices that lead toward the spiritual goal. A primary aim of students should be to meet the highest standards of their worldly occupations: to participate fully and compete equally in professional endeavors, social service, business ventures, community involvement, scholarship, parenting, or any other realms in which they hold responsibility.

I would caution you, however, against letting outer responsibilities become an excuse not to be regular in your practices. Life is short, and if we are not careful, time slips through our fingers. Many people who work for a living also attend night school. They have set aside certain hours each day to pursue their studies; if they did not dedicate this time, they would not earn the degree they seek. Spiritual training also requires time. We all have many responsibilities, and the practices may sometimes seem to divert us from more pressing duties. But capacity grows steadily as the effects of the transmissions are felt. Students who devote time to recitations and meditation (*murāqabah*) often find that they can finish their outer work more efficiently. There is a blessing (*barakah*) associated with the practices that transfers to other activities. For example, one may be struggling to write something. After an hour of effort, one has not finished the first page. One stops to meditate for a while, and then, returning to work, writes what is needed within ten minutes.

Everyday life constantly presents choices that require one to set priorities. The student should choose to give priority to his or her practices. Once I was in the middle of doing recitations in the mosque when it came time for me to meet some important people for the school. I thought, "What should I do: get up and go meet these people, or continue my recitations?" I decided to finish my practices and then go. I soon was absorbed in meditation, and before I knew it, twenty-five minutes had passed. When I again became aware of my surroundings, I noticed the time and thought, "Oh, no!" But upon leaving the mosque, I saw one of the people whom I had wanted to meet walking toward me. He had not planned to go this way, but had changed his route at the last minute. So, I was able to speak with him. When I got closer to home, I encountered the other person I had hoped to see. By giving priority to my practices, I received assistance in completing my work-related duties.

Involve yourself in worldly matters according to the need, just as when you are driving, you direct only as much attention as needed to the weather and road conditions. If you are having problems, one source of your problems may be that you are not putting enough effort into your practices. If you prefer your practices above other engagements, God will look after your needs. Do not think, "I'm too worried to pray or sit in *murāqabah* now. After I've resolved this issue, then I'll give my best to the practices." Give the practices priority, so that with their aid and with the blessings of God, you can rid yourself of troubles more effectively and quickly. If you inculcate this habit, you not only will be less worried about your affairs, but will make more rapid progress on the path.

To increase your sensitivity to the Divine Presence, you may wish to observe a practice known as "heart pause" (*wuqūf al-qalb*). Notice when you start to become engrossed in worldly activities, then stop for a moment, turn to your heart, and think of God. If there is a natural pause in activity, be attentive to your heart and say *Allah* inwardly. Gradually decrease the duration between remembrances. With practice, this periodic remembrance will become regular and automatic, until at last you will be constantly aware of God. You will come to be in the state called *khalwat dar anjuman* (solitude amidst the crowd).

Ḥazrat 'Alī ؓ (d. 661), son-in-law of the Prophet ﷺ, said, "I realized God through the *un*fulfillment of my desires and ambitions." You may be familiar with a similar saying: "Man proposes, God disposes." We all encounter situations where, no matter how hard we try, we cannot succeed. Through such experiences, we come to realize that there exists a will that supersedes individual will. This overarching will is, of course, the will of God. Each of our own wills tussles with God's will all the time. Only through bitter experience do we realize the futility of insisting on having things our way and then see the wisdom in relinquishing any ambition other than God's. The Qur'ān states, *But you shall not will except as God wills, the Cherisher of the world.*[69] We are not enjoined to abandon all efforts on our own behalf. We should do our best, but know that the results are in God's hands. If, despite all possible effort, the outcome is not as desired, we should accept it gladly because God wills it to be so. We should be satisfied with whatever states we face in life.

Always think that God is present with you, sees you, and knows whatever you have in your heart. The daily practices of some orders include reciting *Allāh ḥāḍirī, nāẓirī, shāhidī, ma'ī* ("God is present, observing me, witnessing me, with me"). I remind you again of the saying of the Prophet Muhammad ﷺ: "Adore Allah as though you see Him, and if you do not see Him, know that He nevertheless sees you." If you develop this habit, you will take more care in performing your practices, guard yourself from doing wrong, and have fewer fears and anxieties, for you will not lose sight of God even for a moment. If you become of God, then God will provide you with everything you need, for God is always present, looking after you.

Try to discover those qualities and activities with which God is pleased. One of the most important is service to His creatures. Remember, the path to the love of God passes through the valley of service—service not only to human beings, but to all creatures. Obviously, you cannot serve God directly. However, the Creator is always near to the created, so if you show sympathy and love toward God's creatures, God will have love and sympathy for you.

A dervish wandered here and there for fifteen years, making strenuous efforts to perfect himself. Although he did his best, he could not achieve the realization he sought. One day as he was traveling through a desert, he saw a dog lying on the ground, nearly dead from thirst. The dervish was so moved that he rushed to find water to save the dog's life. At last he located a well, but there was nothing with which to draw water. Finally, he took off his turban and soaked one of its ends. He ran quickly back to the dog and squeezed a few drops from the turban into its mouth. Just then the desert was filled with powerful light, and the dervish received that which had eluded him for fifteen years.

The Prophet Muhammad ﷺ said, "Be merciful to those on earth, and God on high will be merciful to you." Give generously to others; then God on the Throne of Glory will accept you as one of the nearest and dearest.

***

Question 38: Sayyid 'Abd al-Bāri Shah

I gather from your references to Sayyid 'Abd al-Bāri Shah that he played a significant role in your order, but I have not heard of him before. Who was he, and for what is he known?

Although Sayyid[70] 'Abd al-Bāri Shah (r.a.) contributed significantly to Sufi thought and action, little has been written about him. His life holds particular interest for contemporary seekers because he lived and taught in the modern era.

Sayyid 'Abd al-Bāri Shah (r.a.) was born around A.H.1276 (1860 C.E.) at Balgadhi (a village in the Indian state of Bengal). His father was expert in both theology and spiritual science and had mastered alchemy, or what we would call chemistry today. When 'Abd al-Bāri Shah (r.a.) was only six years old, his father passed away, and his mother shouldered full responsibility for raising him.

Sayyid 'Abd al-Bāri Shah's mother not only saw to her son's material needs, but fostered his character through her own model of patience and gratitude. Soon after being widowed, she moved from Balgadhi to Hoogli, near Calcutta, in accordance with the will of her husband. There she spun thread to earn a livelihood. Sayyid 'Abd al-Bāri Shah (r.a.), a considerate child even at that early age, tried to contribute to the family's income by doing menial tasks to help his mother.

After some time, at the request of a relative, the family moved from Hoogli to Naldanga. Here his mother would stay until her last breath, and here the tomb of Sayyid 'Abd al-Bāri Shah (r.a.) would eventually be situated.

Once when Sayyid 'Abd al-Bāri Shah (r.a.) was a child, two or three boys asked him to join them in stealing coconuts. Initially he refused, but when they insisted, he agreed to go along. They reached the trees, and the other boys started picking coconuts. They asked Sayyid 'Abd al-Bāri Shah (r.a.) to stand watch nearby, ready to inform them if anyone approached. A graveyard lay adjacent to the coconut grove. Suddenly, Sayyid 'Abd al-Bāri Shah (r.a.) saw a specter emerge from among the graves and start toward him. "Good boy," the specter said, "you were not born for this purpose." Sayyid 'Abd al-Bāri Shah (r.a.) left his comrades then and there, returning home at once.

Young 'Abd al-Bāri Shah (r.a.) received no formal education. He was admitted to a school but did not care for academic modes of learning, and so he left school and started working at various minor jobs. At last he got a position with a good salary at the railway. He could now have a better life, and also be in the company of friends.

One night, Sayyid 'Abd al-Bāri Shah (r.a.) saw his father in a dream. His father expressed disapproval of the railway job, pointing out that there was much corruption in the workplace. In his heart, Sayyid 'Abd al-Bāri Shah (r.a.) had never been attached to that employment, and upon waking he decided to resign. His Arabic teacher and some of his friends tried to prevent him from resigning; they warned him that he would have trouble finding comparable work. Ignoring their advice, he quit the railway.

Shortly thereafter, he suffered from a dysentery so acute that people thought he might not survive. Again he saw his father in a dream. His father gave him something to eat, from which he ate his fill. When he awoke, he felt better, and within a few days he was completely cured.

These experiences transformed Sayyid ʻAbd al-Bāri Shah (r.a.). He began to devote most of his time to spiritual pursuits. He also started searching for a shaykh.

He received his first initiation at the hand of the Chishtī shaykh Ḥazrat Karīm Bakhsh (r.a.), who was an officer in the survey department and once happened to pass through Balgadhi when making an official visit to Calcutta. During his short stay in Balgadhi, Shaykh Karīm (r.a.) taught Sayyid ʻAbd al-Bāri Shah (r.a.) to observe *pas-an-fas* (awareness of breath). As soon as Sayyid ʻAbd al-Bāri Shah (r.a.) started doing the practice, his heart opened. He found the experience quite fulfilling and began to apply himself even more enthusiastically to the mystical practices. His only regret was that he could not see the shaykh again, for the latter's work did not bring him back to Balgadhi.

One day when Sayyid ʻAbd al-Bāri Shah (r.a.) was engaged in *dhikr* (recitations evoking remembrance of God), there appeared before him Ḥazrat Moinuddīn Chishtī of Ajmer (r.a.) (d. 1236), founder of the Chishtī Order in India. The latter explained that although the initiation from Shaykh Karīm (r.a.) was valid, in the future, he himself would instruct Sayyid ʻAbd al-Bāri Shah (r.a.).[71] From that time forward, Ḥazrat Moinuddīn Chishtī (r.a.) came regularly to impart transmission. "Do not think that it was a matter of vision," Sayyid ʻAbd al-Bāri Shah (r.a.) once told his deputy, Ḥazrat Ḥāmid Ḥasan 'Alawī (r.a.) (d. 1959). "He used to sit with me as you sit now in front of me."

Ḥazrat Moinuddīn Chishtī (r.a.) assisted Sayyid 'Abd al-Bāri Shah (r.a.) through the stations on the path. The latter narrated:

> Whenever I encountered barriers that I lacked the strength to surmount, Moinuddīn Chishtī (r.a.) would lift me with the help of his special being. I would ask, "Ḥazrat, have I now reached the goal of the journey?" He always replied, "No. The goal is still far away"—until finally, one day, he said, "Now you have reached the destination."

When Sayyid 'Abd al-Bāri Shah (r.a.) had completed the Chishtī teachings, Ḥazrat Moinuddīn Chishtī (r.a.) made him a *khalīfah* (deputy) and gave him *ijāzah* (authorization to teach) in the order.

As I have mentioned, recent shaykhs of the Naqshbandī-Mujaddidī line have not employed austerities as a spiritual discipline. Life's circumstances, however, frequently forced austerities on Sayyid 'Abd al-Bāri Shah (r.a.). Although the blessings of God flowed constantly toward him, and Moinuddīn Chishtī (r.a.) regularly granted him spiritual favors, on the worldly plane, his situation was miserable. Whatever money he had continually ran out.

Once when Ramaḍān (the month of fasting) coincided with the rainy season, a day came when Sayyid 'Abd al-Bāri Shah (r.a.) and his wife had only one penny left. With this penny, they bought some grain, which enabled them to carry on for two more days. Finally, not a single coin remained in the house. Looking back on this period, Ḥazrat

Sayyid 'Abd al-Bāri Shah (r.a.) later observed, "I did not fear being tested, but I worried for my wife. I was concerned that she might not bear the strain and would become impatient." But in the accompaniment of great souls, average souls also exhibit greatness. His wife put plain water in a pot on the fire so the neighbors would not suspect that they were starving.

The couple passed two days in this condition. They could break the fast only with sips of water. At such moments, even the best of people may lose hope and become distracted from the path. Ḥazrat Sayyid 'Abd al-Bāri Shah (r.a.), however, devoted himself fully to his practices. He did not stop even to relieve himself. Knowing death could be near, he determined to do as much as he could in his spiritual pursuit. It began raining, and water poured down around him through gaps in the roof. Still, Sayyid 'Abd al-Bāri Shah (r.a.) remained busy with his remembrance of God, or *dhikr*. He put a pot on his head to keep the water off. Whenever the rain ceased for a moment, he would empty the pot, return it to his head, and continue meditating.

It is said that one day when he and his wife were in this sorry state, he was visited in a vision by Ḥazrat 'Alī رضي الله عنه and Ḥazrat Shaykh 'Abd al-Qādir Jīlānī (r.a),[72] dressed in beautiful shining garments and holding unsheathed swords in their hands. They had appeared to Ḥazrat Sayyid 'Abd al-Bāri Shah (r.a.) several times before, but today's visit was a special one. While one caught hold of his right arm, the other took his left, and together they lifted him until he stood on a high platform. They said, "O 'Abd al-Bāri, you shall be a *walī* (friend of God) from this day forward!"

After Ḥazrat Sayyid 'Abd al-Bāri Shah (r.a.) had come out of this state, but while he was still in meditation, a man entered his room and said, "O Ḥazrat Sayyid, this hut's roof is in terrible shape. Please allow me to repair it." Another man stopped by to give him two rupees as a sign of reverence. In brief, the unfavorable times ended. Ḥazrat Sayyid 'Abd al-Bāri Shah (r.a.) and his wife never faced starvation again, although they sometimes went hungry for three or four days in a month.

Each *ṭarīqah* (order) has stories about the *awliyā'* (saints), their spiritual accomplishments, and the honors or positions accorded them. Whether we interpret these accounts literally or metaphorically, they can provide inspiration as we encounter our own challenges on the journey. Such stories also attest to the heights that can be attained by sincere seekers of truth.

One story of Sayyid 'Abd al-Bāri Shah (r.a.) concerns his relationship with his contemporary, the Mujaddidī shaykh Mawlānā Ghulām Salmānī of East Bengal (r.a.) (d. 1912). With the aid of transmissions received from Shaykh Salmānī (r.a.), Sayyid 'Abd al-Bāri Shah (r.a.) illumined within himself each of the ten centers of consciousness (*al-laṭā'if al-'asharah*). He then asked the shaykh to accept him as a *murīd* (disciple). Shaykh Salmānī (r.a.), unlike other teachers of the time, was not fond of taking followers as *murīds*. He refused his student's request, saying, "I have given you the instructions. Now go and devote yourself wholeheartedly to the teachings. God may bless and help you." Sayyid 'Abd al-Bāri Shah (r.a.) was terribly disappointed. As he sat in meditation later, the founder of the Mujaddidī Order, Shaykh Aḥmad Farūqī Sirhindī (r.a.) (d. 1624), appeared in a vision and asked the reason for his grief. After hearing what had happened, Shaykh Ahmad Sirhindi (r.a.) said, "Return to Shaykh Salmānī. This time, he will accept you as a *murīd*." Sayyid 'Abd al-Bāri Shah (r.a.) visited the shaykh and described his conversation with Shaykh Ahmad Sirhindi (r.a.).

After hearing of the incident, Shaykh Salmānī (r.a.) took him as a disciple.

Although outwardly, Sayyid 'Abd al-Bāri Shah (r.a.) was the *murīd* of Ḥazrat Mawlānā Salmānī (r.a.), inwardly, he received transmission from Shaykh Ahmad Sirhindi (r.a.). Through the method of *uwaysī*,[73] the founders of four other orders—Ḥazrat Shaykh 'Abd al-Qādir Jīlānī of Baghdad (r.a.) (d. 1166), Shaykh Abū al-Ḥasan Shādhilī of Alexandria (r.a.) (d. 1258), Ḥazrat Khwājah Bahā'uddīn Naqshband of Bukhara (r.a.) (d. 1389), and the Yemenite saint Ḥazrat Uways al-Qaranī (r.a.) (d. 657)—also made him their deputies and authorized him to teach in their orders.

In sum, Ḥazrat Sayyid 'Abd al-Bāri Shah (r.a.) received permission to initiate and teach students in the Chishtī, Mujaddidī, Qādirī, Shādhilī, Naqshbandī, and Qaranī Orders.

Many of the stories told about Sayyid 'Abd al-Bāri Shah (r.a.) relate to roles he is said to have held within the Sufi spiritual hierarchy. According to one story, there lived in Calcutta an elderly woman who was one of the forty *abdāl* (substitutes[74]). Ḥazrat Sayyid 'Abd al-Bāri Shah (r.a.) sometimes met with her, and when she died, he was asked through his *kashf* (intuitive insight) to carry on her duties as one of the *abdāl*.

Other stories pertain to the position of *al-quṭb al-madār* (the pole of the universe[75]). Many people believed that *al-quṭb al-madār* at this time was Shaykh Abū al-Ḥasan (r.a.) of Mecca,[76] who was known for his powers of transmission. Sayyid 'Abd al-Bāri Shah (r.a.) established a spiritual connection with him, and through this connection, Shaykh Abū al-Ḥasan directed attention to him daily, imparting transmission after transmission to his heart. Sayyid 'Abd al-Bāri Shah (r.a.) reported that sometimes, he met with

Shaykh Abū al-Ḥasan (r.a.) in Mecca, and at other times, Shaykh Abū al-Ḥasan (r.a.) would meet him in India. When Ḥazrat Ḥāmid Ḥasan ʻAlawī (r.a.) heard this, he expressed amazement, for the two men lived thousands of miles apart. But Ḥazrat Sayyid ʻAbd al-Bāri Shah (r.a.) said that in spiritual journeying, space and time do not count.

When Shaykh Abū al-Ḥasan (r.a.) left the body, there was a gathering in the vicinity of the Holy Kaʻbah. The crowd included many great mystics who were candidates for the post of *al-quṭb al-madār*. Sayyid ʻAbd al-Bāri Shah (r.a.) also was present, but thinking himself lowest of all and unfit for the position, he stood behind those who desired it. Then the angel Gabriel ﵇ stepped into the assembly bearing a crown of jewels and pearls. He called the name of Ḥazrat Sayyid ʻAbd al-Bāri Shah (r.a.). The latter rushed to stand before the angel, who—placing the crown upon his head—motioned toward the Kaʻbah and said, "You are the caretaker of this house from this day forward."

Those who knew and followed Ḥazrat Sayyid ʻAbd al-Bāri Shah (r.a.) also thought him to be the *quṭb al-irshād* (pole for spiritual guidance) of the time. Throughout history, only a few select persons have had the privilege of serving as both "poles." It is said that the world never remains without *al-quṭb al-madār*: when one leaves the body, another takes his or her place immediately. But a *quṭb al-irshād* need not be physically present at all times, for the spirit of this "pole" may carry on his or her work even after leaving the body. Seekers may continue to experience the spirit of Sayyid ʻAbd al-Bāri Shah (r.a.) imparting spiritual guidance, although the shaykh passed away more than a century ago.

The concept of unseen spiritual hierarchies is foreign to most people today, and I do not mean to dwell on it. The critical point for modern-day students is that according to Sufi thought, various individuals who have left the body continue to offer guidance and *madad* (assistance) to seekers.

Ḥazrat Sayyid 'Abd al-Bāri Shah (r.a.) felt a special closeness to the earlier master Shaykh 'Abd al-Qādir Jīlānī (r.a.). He would hold up two fingers side by side and say, "He and I are like these fingers. Where he is present, he asks me to join him there." Like Shaykh 'Abd al-Qādir Jīlānī (r.a.), Sayyid 'Abd al-Bāri Shah (r.a.) was reputed to have the ability to award the rank of *walī* to a *sālik* (spiritual traveler).[77] Once he happened upon a grave and stood contemplating it for a long while, apparently out of reverence for the deceased. His companions began to wonder aloud whether the person buried there had been a *walī*. Sayyid 'Abd al-Bāri Shah (r.a.) answered, "He wasn't a *walī* before, but now he is."

Ḥazrat Sayyid 'Abd al-Bāri Shah (r.a.) was also considered to be the *muḥāfiẓ al-'ulūm*: "guardian of the knowledges," meaning protector of both *sharī'ah* (religious or sacred law) and *ṭarīqah* (the mystical path). He was not only afforded this title by others, but lived it personally, exemplifying the inseparability of Islam and Sufism.

Ḥazrat Sayyid 'Abd al-Bāri Shah (r.a.) made important contributions both to the orders in which he was authorized and to Sufism in general. One of the masters of his line, the Indian shaykh Ḥazrat Aḥmad Farūqī Sirhindī (r.a.) (d. 1625), had previously refined the practices of the Naqshbandī Order according to the principle of *indiraj an-nihayah fi'l-bidayah* ("where others end, there marks our beginning"[78]). Ḥazrat Sayyid 'Abd al-Bāri Shah (r.a.) introduced the method of *indiraj an-nihayah fi'l-bidayah* to the rest of the orders in which he was authorized with the consent of their founders.

Sayyid ʻAbd al-Bāri Shah (r.a.) also refined the system of *pīr-i murīdi* (making disciples). He was not satisfied with the prevailing system, which required that an individual become a *murīd* or *murīda* before starting to do the Sufi practices. He put an end to this tradition by permitting aspirants to embark on the spiritual journey without giving *bay'ah* (the pledge of initiation). However, he discovered that after students had completed the sequence of practices that focus on the ten *laṭā'if* (centers of consciousness), they had difficulty proceeding further without entering into discipleship. Today, shaykhs in the line of Sayyid ʻAbd al-Bāri Shah (r.a.) are distinctive in that they do not make *bay'ah* a prerequisite for undertaking the practices. Only after finishing *al-laṭā'if al-'asharah* is a student obliged to make this commitment.

Ḥazrat Sayyid ʻAbd al-Bāri Shah (r.a.) was quite frank with his students. He used to tell them, "There is no need for you to go anywhere else to study. I do not say this from my ego; I say it for your own betterment, in hopes of saving you from distraction." He did not like any special distinction to be accorded to him. Whenever he stayed at his *khalīfah's* (deputy's) house, he said that if anyone inquired about him, that person should simply be told that he was a guest. He seldom uttered harsh words or scolded his students. If he thought it necessary to rebuke them, he would simply say, "You lack *adab* (spiritual courtesy)." He was so merciful that he would immediately add, "I am responsible for your wrong behavior."

Most of his time he devoted to meditation, continuing each sitting for about three hours. He often spent the whole night meditating, yet felt fresh and cheerful in the morning. He loved his students as if they were his sons and daughters. They also loved him very much and were not tempted to leave him for other shaykhs, no matter how great others might be. Once when his water carrier was on the way to the river to fetch water, a person like Khiḍr ﷷ appeared in the distance, beckoning. The water carrier called out, "Why should I come to you? Why shouldn't I go to my own teacher, through whose nearness you are calling me?"

Ḥazrat Sayyid 'Abd al-Bāri Shah (r.a.) received no formal education, but with the help of *al-'ilm al-ladunī*,[79] he could answer questions, quoting books and even citing page and line numbers. The details of every field of knowledge and science stood open before him.

Ḥazrat Sayyid 'Abd al-Bāri Shah (r.a.) was only forty when he left the body and took abode in the heavens. He and his wife had no children.

One day shortly before his passing, Ḥazrat Sayyid 'Abd al-Bāri Shah (r.a.) was making ablution in a corner of his house. As he did so, the thought crossed his mind: "I am a poor man living in solitude, and it seems that this order will remain limited to me alone." The thought saddened him, but then an indication from God lifted his spirits. God made it known to him that by the blessings of the Almighty, this order would spread from East to West and from land to sea. By the grace of God, we can now apprehend signs of the fulfillment of this promise.

***

Question 39: Realizations on the Path

Would you please share some of the realizations experienced by students of Sufism?

The investigations of those who travel the Sufi path are practical and personal, not theoretical, and the resulting realizations are difficult to convey in words. Let me address your question briefly, but please remember that descriptions are limited.

Among students' first realizations is the awareness of a transcendental dimension. Glimpsing aspects of the universe that are inaccessible to intellect, they receive a taste of something beyond material phenomena. A new vision of reality begins to influence their lives and thoughts.

As students awaken the heart and other *laṭā'if* (centers of consciousness), their understanding of self deepens. The rational mind expands, and seekers acquire the illumination necessary for the possibility of seeing all aspects of existence in proper perspective.

Students who continue to do the practices diligently may gain personal experience of the following assertions:

1) The phenomenal world of matter and individual consciousness is only a partial reality.
2) The human being has a self other than the empirical self: the eternal self.
3) One can have direct experience of the Divine through a carefully nurtured interior which is superior to reason and intellect alone.
4) Through faithfully pursuing a discipline with an authorized guide, one can identify one's limited self with the true self.

You asked about realizations, but beyond a certain point, realizations become inseparable from a person's way of being. It becomes clear to students that human beings are not merely slaves to instinct, but have an urge to express higher values and a will capable of controlling their actions. As students begin to see the Divine Presence in everything, they become better able to grasp the meaning of human life—both of their personal lives, and of the collective destiny of humanity. Narrow, ego-centered points of view give way to a broader perspective, encouraging students to make every thought, word, and act a form of *'ibādah* (worship) and *khidmah* (service). They approach a state of consciously desiring good, even in situations involving no personal advantage or external pressure.

Knowing with certainty that everything is governed by the will of God, seekers learn to depend on God, to be patient and accepting. Through the practices they may also receive confirmation that there is life after death. As they recognize that this world is preparation for the next, they are further inspired to adopt a more pious, virtuous lifestyle.

Sufism is a journey from the inner to the outer. Through realizing the self, the seeker realizes God. Through realizing God, the seeker becomes selfless. Step by step, his or her former being becomes transformed, until by the grace of God he or she may attain *fanā'* and *baqā'*: the experience of unity, of being annihilated or consumed in the Divine, of abiding in and with the Almighty.

The experience of unity is not the final realization of the Sufi journey. Those who attain this stage return from it to assist their fellow beings.[80] They are with God and in this world simultaneously, translating the nearness that they feel to the Creator into service to creation. They keep themselves attuned, ready to fulfill the duties and responsibilities that God presents in day-to-day life. The world is like a workshop run by God, and the Sufi at the highest stage of realization is a worker, striving to fill his or her role in the best way possible, relying always on the mercy and blessings of God.

***

Question 40: Sufism and the Future

What role might Sufism play in humanity's future?

To address the direction in which humanity is headed, we need to consider how we got to where we are. Historically, every nation had some concept of a higher power or powers to whom individuals could turn for help amidst the trials of life. The modes through which societies expressed their relationship with the Divine became formalized in religious institutions and rituals. Often, religious structures came to form the very core of the community.

The scientific revolution altered attitudes toward religion. New modes of thought led many individuals to conclude that there was no higher power, for the existence of such could not be rationally proven. Whereas previously, members of a society shared a communal relationship with the Divine, gradually faith came to be seen as a matter of personal choice. Societies became fragmented between the devout and the skeptical, the faithful and the atheistic. Cultures arose that could be called godless—not because they were devoid of religious individuals, but because their central, unifying focus had become material progress rather than spiritual well-being.

Scientific discoveries and inventions increased human knowledge of the universe. But instead of being grateful for and humbled by the gifts of newfound capabilities, human beings exploited them for selfish ends. Consequently, their lives remained devoid of peace and tranquility. Materialism added to humanity's unresolved problems by breeding political and environmental ailments. Greed and cynicism flourished. Conflicts deepened among interests and classes and between the planet and its inhabitants, placing our species on a path toward self-destruction.

Humanity was like an inquisitive, restless child, who—finding herself unsupervised in a huge, magnificent factory—sets the machinery in motion, only to stand back bewildered and helpless as it runs beyond her control. Like the child torn between excitement and terror in the face of the machinery's might, human beings were at once made more comfortable and less secure by their technologies.

The fundamental blunder of this era lay in focusing almost exclusively on external reality and neglecting the world hidden within the human heart. Believing that the only valid sources of knowledge were sensory perception and reason, individuals failed to transcend these modes of knowing. Other dimensions of potential remained untapped. Equipped with imperfect, one-dimensional understandings of the universe, human beings could find no solutions to their ailments.

In the latter half of the twentieth century, more and more people came to realize that science and technology, for all their benefits, could not remedy human ills. Gradually, societies awakened to the need of re-establishing their relationship with the Divine.

Science helped create the dilemmas that now face humanity, and science can help us find a way out. If we conceive of the scientific approach and experimental methods with a wider perspective, we can use them to forge a pathway that will extricate humanity from its suffering and propel it to a state of peace and equilibrium.

The remedy for our global ills must be searched for in human nature itself. The study of external reality alone cannot yield the complete knowledge that is needed to fulfill humanity's highest potentials. Equally important is the exploration of the interior world of the human being. Only by combining both realms of study can we become acquainted with the true destination of humanity and the means for reaching it.

The creeds of religions and spiritual traditions have always pointed to this fundamental truth. Each in its own era has presented a world view and practical guidelines through which humanity could make the most of its God-given potentials. These teachings continue to be sources of wisdom. But we must not allow their interpretations to become static or fixed, for times and circumstances continually change. These teachings worked in their eras because they matched their eras' needs. To work in our children's era, they will need to match our children's needs.

Our order combines inner and outer studies, personal and global concerns, past wisdom and future considerations. Its teachings reflect the conviction that just as atoms have unlimited energy hidden within them, the most evolved form of matter—the human body—is a reservoir of potentialities. The student on the Sufi path searches out this treasure, following a refined scientific approach and experimental method. He or she strives to understand the essential nature of the human being, the universe, and humanity's relationship to the universe in ways that are relevant to today and to tomorrow.

These discoveries will help us find solutions to human beings' individual and collective problems. While material discoveries should continue to be utilized in the service of humanity, Sufism aims to uncover the capabilities within the human self and to utilize them for the benefit of all creation.

Earlier you asked if Sufi teachers use love as a technique. I explained that methods based on love are used more by some shaykhs and less by others. Now that you have asked perhaps the most critical question of all, I will tell you: the hidden power of the self that Sufis seek to utilize is love. It is love that frees human beings from the bonds of narrow-mindedness, materialism, and selfishness. It is love that finds expression in tolerance, sympathy, benevolence, and self-sacrifice. Love motivates, inspires, challenges, and satisfies.

God Alone knows what the future holds. But as humanity evolves generation upon generation, understanding of self and of God will remain our best hope for attuning our attitudes and behavior to the needs of our species, of our planet, and of the universe as a whole. This knowledge alone will enable us to fathom fully the interrelatedness of human existence, the created universe, and the Creator. Through this knowledge, if God wills, our children may bring forth a creed of universal brotherhood and sisterhood, and our children's children may live to see the day when all humanity prospers from God's gifts of unbounded love.

***

NOTES

1. "Ḥazrat" (or "Hadrat") is a title of respect derived from the Arabic word *hadara*, which connotes "being present" or "being in the presence." While the appellation is widely used among Arabic speakers and Muslims, it has special significance in the context of Sufism, a path that aims to increase individuals' awareness of the nearness of God in moment-to-moment life. The Sufi teacher as Ḥazrat may be regarded as one who has attained consciousness of the Divine Presence—who is, metaphorically, present in that Presence—and who can assist seekers in their quest similarly to experience the closeness to God in their lives.

2. In conformance with popular practice, the word "order" is used throughout the text to refer to the lineages of Sufi masters. The original Arabic term for a Sufi lineage is *ṭarīqah*, which means "path or way," not "order." Unlike the religious orders of Christian monastics, the *ṭarīqahs* emerged as "loosely organized bodies of *pīrs* [teachers] and *murīds* [students]" which at their height enjoyed the allegiance of people of diverse backgrounds and life styles, including men and women, rulers and peasants, wandering ascetics and well-established professionals. (Marshall G.S. Hodgson, *The Venture of Islam: Conscience and History in a World Civilization*, Vol. 2 (Chicago: The University of Chicago Press, 1977), pp. 210-222.)

3. Qur'ān XXIV, 58.

4. The terms "Sufism" and *Taṣawwuf*—both derivatives of the Arabic root *ṣ-w-f*—are used interchangeably throughout the text.

5. Muhammad Abdul Haq Ansari, *Sufism and Sharī'ah: A Study of Shaykh Ahmad Sirhindi's Effort to Reform Sufism* (Leicester, UK: The Islamic Foundation, 1986), p. 32.

6. *Fanā'* (literally, to perish, vanish, or be consumed) is the mystical perception of the annihilation of the self and the world in God. The stage following *fanā'* is *baqā'* (literally, to survive, to persist, to be immortal), the experience of subsisting or abiding in God.

7. Qur'ān L, 16.

8. *Murāqabah* refers to attentive observation or watchfulness. However, as a Sufi technical term, it is sometimes translated as "meditation." For the sake of brevity, the latter translation is used in this text.

9. Jalāluddīn Rūmī (r.a.) was born in Balkh, Afghanistan in 1207 or 1208. In adulthood, he settled in Konya, Turkey, where he was a professor of religious sciences as well as mysticism. The Mevlevi lineage of Sufi masters descends from him.

10. The view of human evolution suggested by Rūmī (r.a.) and other Sufis is paralleled in the work of Dr. Jonas Salk, discoverer of the polio vaccine, who observed that human beings "are still undergoing rapid evolution, not at the biological level of complexity, but rather at the metabiological level...The evolutionary need is to increase our breadth of consciousness...[and] to expand our range of choice for the wisest alternatives." (Jonas Salk quoted by Arianna Stassinopoulos in "Courage, Love, Forgiveness," *Parade Magazine*, 4 November 1984: p. 9.)

11. Gurdjieff studied and experimented with the teachings of various spiritual traditions, including several Sufi orders. Evidence suggests that the Naqshbandī Order may have been foremost among the Eastern sources of his own philosophy and teachings. See J.G. Bennett, *Gurdjieff: A Very Great Enigma* (New York: Samuel Weiser, 1973), pp. 55-62. Gurdjieff's studies with Naqshbandī shaykhs (among others) are also mentioned in Rafael Lefort's *The Teachers of Gurdjieff* (Cambridge, MA: ISHK, 1998).

12. See Qur'ān IV, 1: *O humanity! Be conscious of your Lord, Who created you from a single soul, and from it created its mate, and from the two spread abroad a multitude of men and women.*

13. *Awliyā'* literally means "those who are close to; close associates; friends." In a religious context, it implies those who have achieved nearness to or intimacy with the Divine.

14. The Latin root of "sacrifice"—*sacrum facere*, literally "to make sacred"—reflects the transformative potential of sacrifice.

15. Rābi'ah bint Ismā'īl al-'Adawiyyah (r.a.), who taught in Basra, was one of the most prominent early Sufis and has become perhaps the best-known woman Sufi in history. Junayd (r.a.) was a Sufi teacher in Baghdad. Shiblī (r.a.) was his student and successor.

16. For explanations of the methods mentioned here, see the responses to questions 32, 33, and 34.

17. Traditional stories of Sufis' extraordinary powers may be found in A.J. Arberry's *Muslim Saints and Mystics: Episodes from the Tadhkirat al-Auliya' (Memorial of the Saints) by Farīd al-Din 'Attar* (Boston: Routledge & Kegan Paul, 1966) and *Legends of the Sufis: Selections from Menaqibu' l'Arifin* by Shemsu-'d-Din Ahmed, El Eflaki,

third edition, translated by James W. Redhouse (London: Theosophical Publishing House, 1976), among other works.

18. *Kashf* literally means "uncovering"; in Sufi terminology, it refers to the insight or inner vision that the mystic experiences by the grace of God.

19. *An-nafs al-ammārah*—the commanding self—incites human beings towards fulfillment of their basest desires and tendencies. Sufis regard it as the first of seven stages of self that may be achieved through progressive refinement.

20. Muhammad Abdul Haq Ansari, *Sufism and Sharī'ah: A Study of Shaykh Ahmad Sirhindi's Effort to Reform Sufism* (Leicester: The Islamic Foundation, 1986/1406 H), pp. 58-59.

21. Qur'ān II, 143.

22. The ḥadīth ("traditions") are recorded accounts of the statements and actions of the Prophet Muhammad ﷺ. Next to the Qur'ān, they are the second most authoritative source of guidance for Muslims. The Ḥadīth Qudsi are a subset of ḥadīth based on revelations that the Prophet Muhammad ﷺ received from God. They differ from Qur'ānic revelations in that they are stated in the words of the Prophet ﷺ, whereas the contents of the Qur'ān were revealed to the Prophet ﷺ by God through the angel Gabriel ﵇ and reported exactly as revealed.

23. The terms *khānaqāh* (Arabic) and *takīyah* (Turkish; frequently transliterated *tekke*) are synonyms.

24. Qur'ān LVII, 4.

25. Qur'ān L, 16.

26. A.J. Arberry, translator, *Muslim Saints and Mystics: Episodes from the Tadhkirat al-Auliya' (Memorial of the Saints) by Farīd al-Din 'Attar* (Boston: Routledge & Kegan Paul, 1966), p. 51.

27. Ibid.

28. *And indeed within every community have We raised up a messenger, [saying] "Serve Allah and shun evil"* (Qur'ān XVI, 36).

29. The Arabic term *nabī*—translated into English as "prophet"—has broader connotations than corresponding terms in the Torah or Bible. From an Islamic point of view, the prophets include all the righteous leaders sent by God to teach belief in One God and to enjoin virtuous conduct. The first prophet was Adam ﵇ and the last was Muhammad ﷺ. Countless prophets lived between these two: among them, the Qur'ān mentions Jesus ﵇, Moses ﵇, Abraham ﵇, Isaac ﵇, Ishmael ﵇, Jacob ﵇, Joseph ﵇, David ﵇, and Solomon ﵇. The Qur'ān also refers to

other prophets who are not named (Qur'ān XL, 78). Muhammad ﷺ is reported to have said that there were 120,000 prophets in all.

30. G.N. Jalbani, *Teachings of Shah Waliyullah of Delhi*, 3rd ed. (Lahore: Sh. Muhammad Ashraf, 1979), pp. 125-133.

31. Qur'ān II, 256.

32. The works cited are Reynold Alleyne Nicholson's *Studies in Islamic Mysticism* (Delhi: Idarah-i Adabiyat-i, 1981) and Louis Massignon's *Essay on the Origins of the Technical Language of Islamic Mysticism (Essai sur les Origines de Lexique Technique dela Mystique Musulmane)*, translated by Benjamin Clark (Notre Dame, IN: University of Notre Dame Press, 1997). Further elucidation of this topic may be found in Martin Lings' *What is Sufism* (Cambridge, UK: Islamic Texts Society, 1993).

33. Martin Lings, *Muhammad: His Life Based on the Earliest Sources* (Kuala Lumpur: A.S. Nordeen, 1983), pp. 43 and 211.

34. Qur'ān LXXIII, 20.

35. Abū Bakr ؓ was both the companion and father-in-law of the Prophet Muhammad ﷺ. In 622 C.E., he accompanied the Prophet ﷺ on the *hijrah.* The incident mentioned here took place as the two were hiding in a cave to evade pursuing enemies—hence the need for *silent* recitations. Following the death of the Prophet ﷺ in 632 C.E., Abū Bakr ؓ was selected as the first caliph of the Muslim community. The Naqshbandī and Mujaddidī orders trace their lineage to the Prophet ﷺ through Abū Bakr ؓ.

36. Ḥazrat 'Alī ؓ, the cousin (and later son-in-law) of the Prophet Muhammad ﷺ, was among the first people to embrace the message of Islam. 'Alī ؓ received spiritual instruction directly from the Prophet ﷺ as a member of his household (the *ahl al-bayt*), and it is through 'Alī ؓ that the Shādhilī, Chishtī, and Qādirī orders trace their lineage to the Prophet ﷺ. In addition, 'Alī ؓ served as caliph of the Muslim community from 656 to 661.

37. Annemarie Schimmel, *Mystical Dimensions of Islam* (Chapel Hill: University of North Carolina Press, 1975), pp. 169 and 218-221.

38. *Ṭarīqah* literally means "way or path." See footnote 2 for further clarification.

39. See, for example, J. Spencer Trimingham, *The Sufi Orders in Islam* (Oxford, UK: Oxford University Press, 1998); Arthur F. Buehler, *Sufi Heirs of the Prophet: The Indian Naqshbandīyya and the Rise of the Mediating Sufi Shaykh* (Columbia, SC: University of South Carolina Press, 1998); Muhammad Hisham Kabbani, *The Naqshbandī Sufi*

Way: History and Guidebook of the Saints of the Golden Chain (Chicago: Kazi Publications, 1995); and Hasan Lutfi Shushud, *Masters of Wisdom of Central Asia (Hacegan Hanedani)*, translated by Muhtar Holland (North Yorkshire, UK: Coombe Springs Press, 1983).

40. Khwājah Bahā'uddīn Naqshband's (r.a.) contributions to Sufism are discussed further in response to question 32.

41. *The School of the Shadhdhuliyyah, Volume One: ORISONS*, first edition, translated by Ma'ddawi az-Zirr and 'Abdullah Nur ad-Din Durkee (Alexandria, Egypt: Daru-l-Kutub, 1991), p. 43.

42. According to the doctrine of unity of being (*waḥdat al-wujūd*), God is One and all that exists is God. The disciples of the Andalucian master Ibn 'Arabī (r.a.) (d. 1148) who put forward this view argued that to regard anything in creation as other than God is to see duality where none exists. Proponents of *waḥdat al-wujūd* define the highest stage of realization in terms of unitive experience—becoming fully absorbed in contemplation of the All-Embracing Truth and Oneness that is God.

In contrast, the doctrine of unity of being in vision (*waḥdat ash-shuhūd*) holds that the mystic sees only the One God, but that seeing only God does not negate the existence of all else. God's creation is not the same as God. From this point of view, complete absorption in God is not the ultimate stage of realization; rather, the fully realized human being returns from the state of unity to serve his or her fellow seekers.

For a detailed discussion of these concepts and their implications for the Sufi's experience of the Divine, see Muhammad Abdul Haq Ansari's *Sufism and Sharī'ah: A Study of Shaykh Ahmad Sirhindi's Effort to Reform Sufism* (Leicester: The Islamic Foundation, 1986), pp. 37-56 and 101-117.

43. *Iḥsān* ranks with Islam and *īmān* (faith) as a cornerstone of Islamic life.

44. Qur'ān XLIX, 14.

45. Qur'ān IV, 136.

46. A *madh'hab* is an Islamic school of law. There are four main *madh'habs* within the Sunnī branch of Islam: Mālikī, Ḥanbalī, Hanafī, and Shafi'ī. Shi'a Muslims follow the 'Ja'farī *madh'hab.*

47. Muhammad Hisham Kabbani, "What the Scholars Say about Taṣawwuf," *The Muslim Magazine*, April 1998: pp. 50-51.

48. Khiḍr ﷺ is a mystic sage mentioned in the Qur'ān (XVIII, 65-82) and often referred to as the patron saint of the Sufis.

49. Bābā Farīd (r.a.) (full name Farīduddīn Ganj-i Shakar) later became Bakhtiyar Kaki's (r.a.) deputy. He lived and taught in Ajodhan (present-day Pak Pattan, Pakistan), where he died in 1265.

50. Abū'l-Qāsim al-Qushayrī, *Sufi Book of Spiritual Ascent (al-Risala al-Qushayriya)*, translated by Rabia Harris, edited by Laleh Bakhtiar (Chicago, IL: ABC International Group, 1997), p. 298.

51. Qur'ān XCV, 4-5. The complete verse reads, *Surely We created the human being of the best stature, then We reduced him to the lowest of the low, except those who believe and do good works, for they shall have a reward unfailing.*

52. Mir Valiuddin, *Contemplative Disciplines in Sufism* (London: East West Publications, 1980), p. 71.

53. For more information on *indirāj an-nihāyah fi'l-bidāyah*, see the response to question 32.

54. Arthur F. Buehler, *Sufi Heirs of the Prophet: The Indian Naqshbandīyya and the Rise of the Mediating Sufi Shaykh* (Columbia, SC: University of South Carolina Press, 1998), pp. 99-100.

55. Shāh Walīullāh, *The Sacred Knowledge of the Higher Functions of the Mind (Altaf al-quds)*, translated by G.N. Jalbani, edited by David Pendlebury (London: Octagon Press, 1982), pp. 3-4; concluding passage is Qur'ān XII, 38.

56. No single English term can satisfactorily convey the implications of *tawajjuh*. Literally, the word means "attention." Other connotations derive from the verb form *wajjuha*, which means "to direct, steer, guide, or channel," as well as "to face, to turn one's attention." Another form, *tawjeeh*, means "instruction, transfer, or conveyance." *Tawajjuh* therefore implies that the student turns his or her attention toward the heart and toward the sources of the guidance that he or she seeks to receive; in return, the shaykh conveys guidance, direction, and instruction into the heart of the seeker.

57. Muhammad Asad, *The Message of the Qur'ān* (Gibralter: Dar al-Andalus, 1980), p. 963. The first verses of Qur'ān imparted to the Prophet Muhammad ﷺ were: *Read: In the Name of your Lord Who created—created the human being from clots of blood. Read: And your Lord is the Most Generous One, Who has taught by the pen—taught the human being what he did not know* (XCV1, 1-5).

58. This exchange is all the more significant given that 'Umar ؓ had at one time staunchly opposed the Prophet ﷺ and his followers in Mecca. Following the deaths of the Prophet ﷺ (d. 632) and of the first caliph, Abū Bakr ؓ (d. 634), 'Umar ؓ was appointed caliph. He led the Muslim community until his assassination in 644.

59. "Anniversary" in this context means the date of death, understood by Sufis as marking the beginning of the soul's reunion with the Beloved.

60. As previously mentioned (see the responses to questions 22 and 27), the statement "Adore Allah as if you are seeing Him..." defines *iḥsān.*

61. Qur'ān XX, 14.

62. Muhammad Mahmood Ali Qutbi, *Fragrance of Sufism* (Karachi: Royal Book Co., 1993), pp. 21-23.

63. Shaykhul Ḥadīth Maulana Muhammad Zakariyya, "Virtues of *Dhikr*," *Fazail-e-A'mal*, Vol. I, translated by Abdul Rashid Arshad (New Delhi: Idara Asha'at-e-Diniyat, 1990), pp. 570-571.

64. Ibid., p. 572.

65. The relationship between Shaykh Bahā'uddin Naqshband (r.a.) and Shaykh 'Abd al-Khāliq Ghujduwāni (r.a.) (who pre-deceased him by two centuries) is an example of an *uwaysī* connection—that is, a bond through which a living student may receive instruction from a shaykh who has departed the physical body. For more information, see footnote 71.

66. Qur'ān III, 191.

67. Qur'ān LXII, 10.

68. Qur'ān II, 152.

69. Qur'ān LXXXI, 29.

70. The honorific "Sayyid" indicates that 'Abdul Bāri Shah (r.a.) was a descendant of the Prophet Muhammad ﷺ.

71. Sufis use the term *uwaysī* to describe a spiritual connection through which a living student receives blessings and guidance from a deceased shaykh (or, in some cases, the Prophet Muhammad ﷺ). The concept originates in the story of Uways al-Qaranī ؓ, a Yemenite living at the time of the Prophet Muhammad ﷺ, who never had the opportunity to meet the Prophet ﷺ, yet made contact with him through visions. (Shaykh Fadhlalla Haeri, *The Elements of Sufism* (Rockport, MA: Element Books, 1993), p. 40, and Arthur F. Buehler, *Sufi Heirs of the Prophet: The Indian Naqshbandīyya and the Rise of the Mediating Sufi Shaykh* (Columbia, SC: University of South Carolina Press, 1998), pp. 88-89.)

72. Ḥazrat 'Alī ؓ (d. 661), son-in-law of the Prophet Muhammad ﷺ and fourth caliph of the Muslim community, is the spiritual teacher through whom the Shādhilī, Chishtī, and Qādirī orders trace their lineage to the Prophet ﷺ. Shaykh 'Abd al-Qādir Jīlānī (r.a.) (d. 1166), a prominent Sufi master of Baghdad, founded the Qādirī Order.

73. *Uwaysī* refers to a spiritual connection, typically between a departed master and an aspirant or shaykh. For more details, see footnote 71.

74. The *abdāl* are traditionally identified as forty (or seven, according to some authors) perfected mystics whose blessings help to ensure the world's well being. They form one of several tiers of saints centered around a *quṭb*, or spiritual pole or axis. Through these tiers the spiritual bounties of God are said to flow to humanity. When one of the *abdāl* passes on, another saint replaces ("substitutes" for) him or her, keeping the number of *abdāl* constant. (Annemarie Schimmel, *Mystical Dimensions of Islam* (Chapel Hill: University of North Carolina Press, 1975), pp. 200-203; Arthur F. Buehler, *Sufi Heirs of the Prophet: The Indian Naqshbandīyya and the Rise of the Mediating Sufi Shaykh* (Columbia, SC: University of South Carolina Press, 1998), pp. 117-118.)

75. *Qutb* (pole) refers to a position in the Islamic Sufi spiritual hierarchy higher than that of the *abdāl.*

76. The nineteenth-century shaykh Abū al-Ḥasan (r.a.) of Mecca is not to be confused with Shaykh Abū al-Ḥasan Shādhilī (r.a.) (d. 1258), who lived more than six centuries earlier and is buried in Upper Egypt.

77. All Muslims accept that the *ahl al-bayt* (family of the Prophet ﷺ) enjoyed a special link to the Prophet ﷺ and his teachings. Similarly, Sufis look to the *awliyā'* as having achieved such nearness to God that they are able to lift the souls of others to a station of saintliness through just a glance or word.

78. This principle is explained in response to question 32.

79. *Al-'ilm al-ladunī* refers to knowledge which is not learned, but is projected into the tranquil mind of a Sufi from another plane of being.

80. Muhammad Abdul Haq Ansari, *Sufism and Sharī'ah: A Study of Shaykh Ahmad Sirhindi's Effort to Reform Sufism* (Leicester, UK: The Islamic Foundation, 1986), pp. 32-37, 44-45.

APPENDIX A

Shajarahs (Lineage Trees) of the Mujaddidī, Naqshbandī, Qādirī, Chishtī, and Shādhilī Orders

The Prophe

The Caliph Abū Bakr aṣ-Ṣiddīq ﷺ

Naqshbandī Silsila

Ḥaḍrat Salmān Fārsī ﷺ
Ḥaḍrat Qāsim ibn Muḥammad ibn Abī Bakr (r.a.)
Ḥaḍrat Imām Jā'far aṣ-Ṣādiq (r.a.)
Ḥaḍrat Shaykh Abū Yazīd Tayfūr Bisṭāmī (r.a.)
Ḥaḍrat Abū'l-Ḥasan 'Alī ibn Aḥmad Kharaqānī (r.a.)
Ḥaḍrat Abū'Alī Fārmadī Ṭūsī (r.a.)
Ḥaḍrat Abū Ya'qūb Yūsuf Hamadānī (r.a.)
Ḥaḍrat Khwājah 'Abd al-Khāliq Ghujduwānī (r.a.)
Ḥaḍrat Mawlānā 'Ārif Rīwgarī (r.a.)
Ḥaḍrat Khwājah Maḥmūd Abū al-Khayr Anjīr Faghnawī (r.a.)
Ḥaḍrat 'Azīzān 'Alī Rāmitanī (r.a.)
Ḥaḍrat Mawlānā Muḥammad Bābā Sammāsī (r.a.)
Ḥaḍrat Sayyid Amīr Kulāl (r.a.)
Ḥaḍrat Khwājah Muḥammad Bahā'uddīn Shāh Naqshband (r.a.)

Ḥaḍrat Khwājah 'Alā'uddīn al-'Aṭṭār (r.a.)
Ḥaḍrat Mawlānā Ya'qūb Charkhī (r.a.)
Ḥaḍrat Khwājah 'Ubaydullāh Aḥrār (r.a.)
Ḥaḍrat Mawlānā Muḥammad az-Zāhid Wakhshī (r.a.)
Ḥaḍrat Mawlānā Darwīsh Muḥammad (r.a.)
Ḥaḍrat Mawlānā Muḥammad Khwājah Amkanagī (r.a.)
Ḥaḍrat Khwājah Muḥammad Bāqībillāh (r.a.)
Ḥaḍrat Imām Rabbānī Shaykh Aḥmad Farūqī Sirhindī (r.a.)

Mujaddidī Silsila

Ḥaḍrat Ādam Banūrī (r.a.)
Ḥaḍrat Sayyid 'Abdullāh Akbarābādī (r.a.)
Ḥaḍrat Shāh 'Abd ar-Raḥīm (r.a.)
Ḥaḍrat Shāh Walīullāh (r.a.)
Ḥaḍrat Shāh 'Abd al-'Azīz (r.a.)
Ḥaḍrat Sayyid Aḥmad Shahīd (r.a.)
Ḥaḍrat Ṣūfī Nūr Muḥammad (r.a.)
Ḥaḍrat Ṣūfī Fātiḥ 'Alī Uwaysī (r.a.)
Ḥaḍrat Mawlānā Ghulām Salmānī (r.a.)

Shādhilī Silsila

Ḥaḍrat Imām Ḥusayn ﷺ
Ḥaḍrat Shaykh Muḥammad Jārbadī (r.a.)
Ḥaḍrat Shaykh Sa'īd Qīrwānī (r.a.)
Ḥaḍrat Shaykh Fatiḥ Mas'ūdī (r.a.)
Ḥaḍrat Shaykh Abū al-Qāsim Mīrwānī (r.a.)
Ḥaḍrat Shaykh Abū Is'ḥāq Ibrāhīm Baṣrī (r.a.)
Ḥaḍrat Shaykh Quṭbuddīn Mahmūd Qazwīnī (r.a.)
Ḥaḍrat Shaykh Shamsuddīn (r.a.)
Ḥaḍrat Shaykh Tājuddīn (r.a.)
Ḥaḍrat Shaykh Abū al-Ḥasan 'Alī (r.a.)
Ḥaḍrat Shaykh Taqīuddīn Ṣūfī (r.a.)
Ḥaḍrat Shaykh Sharafuddīn Madanī (r.a.)
Ḥaḍrat Shaykh 'Abd as-Salām ibn Mashīsh (r.a.)
Ḥaḍrat Shaykh Nūruddīn Abū al-Ḥasan Shādhilī (r.a.)

Muḥammad ﷺ

The Caliph Ḥaḍrat ʻAlī ibn Abī Ṭālib

Chishtī Silsila

Ḥaḍrat Ḥasan Baṣrī (r.a.)
Ḥaḍrat Abū al-Faḍl ʻAbd al- Wāḥid ibn Zayd (r.a.)
Ḥaḍrat Abū al-Fayḍ Fuḍayl ibn ʻIyāḍ (r.a.)
Ḥaḍrat Ibrāhīm ibn Adham Balkhī (r.a.)
Ḥaḍrat Khwājah Sadīduddīn Ḥudhayfah Marʻashī (r.a.)
Ḥaḍrat Khwājah Amīnuddīn Abū Hubayrah Baṣrī (r.a.)
Ḥaḍrat Khwājah Mamshād ʻUlw Dīnawarī (r.a.)
Ḥaḍrat Khwājah Abū Is'ḥāq Shāmī Chishtī (r.a.)
Ḥaḍrat Khwājah Abū Aḥmad ibn Farasnafa (r.a.)
Ḥaḍrat Khwājah Abū Muḥammad ibn Aḥmad (r.a.)
Ḥaḍrat Khwājah Abū Yūsuf Chishtī (r.a.)
Ḥaḍrat Muḥammad Mawdūd Chishtī (r.a.)
Ḥaḍrat Ḥajjī Sharīf Zindānī (r.a.)
Ḥaḍrat Khwājah ʻUthmān Harvanī (r.a.)
Ḥaḍrat Khwājah Muʻīnuddīn Chishtī (r.a.)
Ḥaḍrat Quṭbuddīn Bakhtiyār Kākī (r.a.)
Ḥaḍrat Farīduddīn Masʻūd Ganj-i Shakar (r.a.)
Ḥaḍrat Khwājah Niẓāmuddīn Awliyā' (r.a.)
Ḥaḍrat Naṣīruddīn Chirāgh-i Delhī (r.a.)
Ḥaḍrat Kamāluddīn ʻAllāma (r.a.)
Ḥaḍrat Sirājuddīn (r.a.)
Ḥaḍrat ʻIlmuddīn (r.a.)
Ḥaḍrat Maḥmūd (r.a.)
Ḥaḍrat Jamāluddīn (r.a.)
Ḥaḍrat Ḥasan (r.a.)
Ḥaḍrat Muḥammad (r.a.)
Ḥaḍrat Muḥammad Yaḥyā Madanī (r.a.)
Ḥaḍrat Mawlānā Kalīmullāh Jahānābādī (r.a.)
Ḥaḍrat Mawlānā Niẓāmuddīn (r.a.)
Ḥaḍrat Mawlānā Fakhruddīn (r.a.)
Ḥaḍrat Mawlānā Shāh Niyāz Aḥmad (r.a.)
Ḥaḍrat Mawlānā Shaykh Miskīn (r.a.)
Ḥaḍrat Mawlānā Nijābat ʻAlī Shāh (r.a.)
Ḥaḍrat Abū Ḥāmid Karīm Bakhsh (r.a.)

Qādirī Silsila

Ḥaḍrat Imām Ḥusayn
Ḥaḍrat Imām ʻAlī Zayn al-ʻĀbidīn (r.a.)
Ḥaḍrat Imām Muḥammad Bāqir (r.a.)
Ḥaḍrat Imām Jāʻfar aṣ-Ṣādiq (r.a.)
Ḥaḍrat Imām Mūsā al-Kāẓim (r.a.)
Ḥaḍrat Imām Mūsā Riḍā (r.a.)
Ḥaḍrat Maʻrūf Karkhī (r.a.)
Ḥaḍrat Sarī Saqaṭī (r.a.)
Ḥaḍrat Junayd Baghdādī (r.a.)
Ḥaḍrat Shaykh Abū Bakr Shiblī (r.a.)
Ḥaḍrat Shaykh ʻAbd al-ʻAzīz Tamīmī (r.a.)
Ḥaḍrat Abū al-Faḍl Abū al-Wāḥid Tamīmī (r.a.)
Ḥaḍrat Abū al-Faraḥ Tarṭūsī (r.a.)
Ḥaḍrat Abū al-Ḥasan Farshī (r.a.)
Ḥaḍrat Abū Saʻīd al-Mubārak Mukharrimī (r.a.)
Ḥaḍrat Shaykh ʻAbd al-Qādir Jīlānī (r.a.)

Ḥaḍrat Sayyid ʻAbd al-Bāri Shāh (r.a.)
Ḥaḍrat Ḥāfiẓ Ḥāmid Ḥasan ʻAlawī (r.a.)
Ḥaḍrat Muḥammad Saʻīd Khān (r.a.)
Ḥaḍrat Azad Rasool

The appendices document the lines of teachers through whom the authorș predecessors traced their spiritual descent from the Prophet Muhammad ﷺ. For clarityș sake, the numerous parallel branches that have extended from shaykhs with multiple khalifahs (deputies) are not shown.

Direct connection

uwasi connection (by internal transmission)

APPENDIX B

Shajarahs (Lineage Trees) with Sufi Masters' Dates and Locations

Naqshbandī-Mujaddidī	Dates	Place Born and/or Lived	Place Died
The Prophet Muḥammad ﷺ	570-632 (51 B.H. - 10 A.H.)	Mecca, Medina	Medina
The Caliph Abū Bakr aṣ-Ṣiddīq ﷺ	571-634 (50 B.H. - 13 A.H.)	Mecca, Medina	Medina
Salmān Fārisī ﷺ	d. 655 (356)	Isfahan (Persia), Syria, Medina, Ctesiphon (Persia)	Jerusalem
Ḥaḍrat Qāsim ibn Muḥammad ibn Abī Bakr (r.a.)	655-726 (37-108)	Medina	Qudayd (near Medina)
Ḥaḍrat Imām Jā'far aṣ-Ṣādiq (r.a.)	702-765 (83-148)	Medina	Medina
Ḥaḍrat Shaykh Abū Yazīd Tayfūr Bisṭāmī (r.a.)	d. 875 (261)	Syria, Persia	Damascus or Bistam (Persia)
Ḥaḍrat Abū al-Ḥasan 'Alī ibn Aḥmad Kharaqānī (r.a.)	953 or 962/64–1033 (341 or 350/52-425)	Kharaqan (near Bistam, in Khurasan, Persia)	Kharaqan
Ḥaḍrat Abū 'Alī al-Fārmadī Ṭūsī (r.a.)	d. 1084 (477)	Khurasan (Persia)	Farmad (near Tus, Persia)
Ḥaḍrat Abū Ya'qūb Yūsuf al-Hamadānī (r.a.)	1048-1140 (440-535)	Buzanjird (near Hamadan, Persia), Baghdad, Isfahan, Bukhara (Central Asia)	Merv (Persia)
Ḥaḍrat Khwājah 'Abd al-Khāliq Ghujduwānī (r.a.)	d. 1179 (575) or 1220 (617)	Ghujduwān (near Bukhara), Bukhara	
Ḥaḍrat Mawlānā 'Ārif Rīwgarī (r.a.)	d. 1219 (616) or 1239 (636)	Bukhara	Riwakar (near Bukhara)
Ḥaḍrat Khwājah Mahmūd Abū al-Khayr Anjīr Faghnawī (r.a.)	d. 1245 (643) or 1272 (670) or 1317 (717)	Bukhara	Qilit (near Bukhara)
Ḥaḍrat 'Azīzān 'Alī Rāmitanī (r.a.)	d. 1239 (636) or 1315 (715) or 1321 (721)	Bukhara	Khwarazm (Central Asia)
Ḥaḍrat Mawlānā Muḥammad Bābā Sammāsī (r.a.)	d. 1340 (740) or 1354 (755)	Bukhara	Samas (near Bukhara)
Ḥaḍrat Sayyid Amīr Kulāl (r.a.)	d. 1370 (772)	Bukhara	Sukhar (near Bukhara)
Ḥaḍrat Khwājah Muḥammad Bahā'uddīn Shāh Naqshband (r.a.)	1317-1389 (717-791)	Bukhara	Bukhara
Ḥaḍrat Khwājah 'Alā'uddīn al-'Aṭṭār (r.a.)	d. 1400 (803)	Khwarazm (Central Asia)	Jaganyan (near Bukhara)
Ḥaḍrat Mawlānā Ya'qūb al-Charkhī (r.a.)	d. 1447 (851)	Charkh (Afghanistan), Central Asia	Hisar (near Dushanbe, Tajikistan)
Ḥaḍrat Khwājah 'Ubaydullāh Aḥrār (r.a.)	1404-1490 (804-896)	Tashkent (Central Asia)	Kaman Kashan near Samarqand
Ḥaḍrat Mawlānā Muḥammad az-Zāhid Wakhshī (r.a.)	d. 1529 (936)	Central Asia	Samarqand
Ḥaḍrat Mawlānā Darwīsh Muḥammad (r.a.)	d. 1562 (970)	Central Asia	Samarqand
Ḥaḍrat Mawlānā Muḥammad Khwājah al-Amkanagī (r.a.)	d. 1600 (1008)	Bukhara	Shash (Afghanistan)
Ḥaḍrat Khwājah Muḥammad Bāqībillāh (r.a.)	1564-1603 (972-1012)	Kabul, Delhi	Delhi

Ḥaḍrat Imām Rabbānī Shaykh Aḥmad Fārūqī Sirhindī (r.a.)	564-1625 (972-1034)	Sirhind (India)	Sirhind
Ḥaḍrat Ādam Banūrī (r.a.)	d. 1643 (1053)		Medina
Ḥaḍrat Sayyid 'Abdullāh Akbarābādī (r.a.)			Agra (India)
Ḥaḍrat Shāh 'Abd ar-Raḥīm (r.a.)	d. 1719 (1131/32)	Delhi	Delhi
Ḥaḍrat Shāh Walīullāh (r.a.)	1702-1762 (1114-1176)	Delhi, Medina	Delhi
Ḥaḍrat Shāh 'Abd al-'Azīz (r.a.)	1746-1824 (1159-1239)	Delhi	Delhi
Ḥaḍrat Sayyid Aḥmad Shahīd (r.a.)	1786-1831 (1201-1246)	Bareilly (India), Delhi	Balakot (India)
Ḥaḍrat Ṣūfī Nūr Muḥammad (r.a.)			Nizamur (Bangladesh)
Ḥaḍrat Ṣūfī Fātiḥ 'Alī Uwaysī (r.a.)	d. 1886 (1304)		Calcutta
Ḥaḍrat Mawlānā Ghulām Salmānī (r.a.)	d. 1912 (1330)		Phuphura (West Bengal)
Ḥaḍrat Sayyid 'Abd al-Bārī Shāh (r.a.)	1859-1900 (1276-1318)	Balgadhi (Bengal), Calcutta	Bandel (West Bengal)
Ḥaḍrat Ḥāfiẓ Ḥāmid Ḥasan 'Alawī (r.a.)	1871/72-1959 (1288-1378)		Gonda (India)
Ḥaḍrat Muḥammad Sa'īd Khān (r.a.)	1907-1976 (1325-1396)		Azamgarh (India)
Ḥaḍrat Azad Rasool	b. 1921 (1339)	Rajistan (India)	

Shādhilī	Dates	Place Born or Lived	Place Died
The Prophet Muḥammad ﷺ	570-632 (51 B.H. - 10 A.H.)	Mecca, Medina	Medina
The Caliph Ḥaḍrat 'Alī ibn Abī Ṭalib ؓ	c. 598-661 (c. 24 B.H. - 41 A.H.)	Mecca, Medina	Kūfah
Ḥaḍrat Imām Ḥusayn ؓ	626-680 (4-60)	Medina	Karbalā'
Ḥaḍrat Shaykh Muḥammad Jārbadī (r.a.)			
Ḥaḍrat Shaykh Sa'īd Qīrwānī (r.a.)			
Ḥaḍrat Shaykh Fatiḥ Mas'ūdī (r.a.)			
Ḥaḍrat Shaykh Abū al-Qāsim Mīrwānī (r.a.)			
Ḥaḍrat Shaykh Abū Isḥāq Ibrāhīm Baṣrī (r.a.)			
Ḥaḍrat Shaykh Quṭbuddīn Mahmūd Qazwīnī (r.a.)			
Ḥaḍrat Shaykh Shamsuddīn (r.a.)			
Ḥaḍrat Shaykh Tājuddīn (r.a.)			
Ḥaḍrat Shaykh Abū al-Ḥasan 'Alī (r.a.)			
Ḥaḍrat Shaykh Taqīuddīn Ṣūfī (r.a.)			
Ḥaḍrat Shaykh Sharafuddīn Madanī (r.a.)			
Ḥaḍrat Shaykh 'Abd as-Salām ibn Mashīsh (r.a.)	d. 1228 (625)	Fez	southeast of Tetuan (Morocco)
Ḥaḍrat Shaykh Nūruddīn Abū al-Ḥasan Shādilī (r.a.)	1196-1258 (592-656)	Ghumara (Morocco), Fez, Alexandria (Egypt)	Humaythra (Egypt)
Ḥaḍrat Sayyid 'Abd al-Bārī Shāh (r.a.)	1859-1900 (1276-1318)	Balgadhi (Bengal), Calcutta	Bandel (West Bengal)
Ḥaḍrat Ḥāfiẓ Ḥāmid Ḥasan 'Alawī (r.a.)	1871/72-1959 (1288-1378)		Gonda (India)
Ḥaḍrat Muḥammad Sa'īd Khān (r.a.)	1907-1976 (1325-1396)		Azamgarh (India)
Ḥaḍrat Azad Rasool	b. 1921 (1339)	Rajistan (India)	

Chishtī	Dates	Place Born or Lived	Place Died
The Prophet Muḥammad ﷺ	570-632 (51 B.H. - 10 A.H.)	Mecca, Medina	Medina
The Caliph Ḥaḍrat 'Alī ibn Abī Ṭalib ؓ	c. 598-661 (c. 24 B.H. - 41 A.H.)	Mecca, Medina	Kufah
Ḥaḍrat Ḥasan Baṣrī (r.a.)	642-728 (21-110)	Medina	Basrah
Ḥaḍrat Abū al-Faḍl 'Abd al-Wāḥid ibn Zayd (r.a.)	d. 793 (177)		
Ḥaḍrat Abū al-Fayḍ Fuḍayl ibn 'Iyāḍ (r.a.)	d. 803 (187)		Makkah
Ḥaḍrat Ibrāhīm ibn Adham Balkhī (r.a.)	d. 777/9 (160/2)	Balkh	
Ḥaḍrat Khwājah Sadīduddīn Ḥudhayfah Mar'ashī (r.a.)			
Ḥaḍrat Khwājah Amīnuddīn Abū Hubayrah Baṣrī (r.a.)			Basrah
Ḥaḍrat Khwājah Mamshād 'Ulw Dīnawarī (r.a.)			Dinawar (Persia), Basrah
Ḥaḍrat Khwājah Abū Isḥāq Shāmī Chishtī (r.a.)	d. 940 or 966 (329 or 366)	Syria, Chisht (Afghanistan)	Akka (Syria)
Ḥaḍrat Khwājah Abū Aḥmad ibn Farasnafa (r.a.)	873/4-966 (260-355)	Chisht	Chisht
Ḥaḍrat Khwājah Abū Muḥammad ibn Aḥmad (r.a.)	d. 1020 (411)	Chisht	Chisht
Ḥaḍrat Khwājah Abū Yūsuf Chishtī (r.a.)	985-1066/7 (375-459)	Chisht	Chisht
Ḥaḍrat Muḥammad Mawdūd Chishtī (r.a.)	d. 1133 (527) or 1181/82 (577)	Herat, Balkh, Bukhara	
Ḥaḍrat Ḥajjī Sharīf Zindānī (r.a.)			
Ḥaḍrat Khwājah 'Uthmān Harvanī (r.a.)		Harvan (Nishapur, Persia)	
Ḥaḍrat Khwājah Mu'īnuddīn Chishtī (r.a.)	1142-1236 (537-633)	Seistan (Persia), Ajmer (India), Delhi	Ajmer
Ḥaḍrat Quṭbuddīn Bakhtiyār Kākī (r.a.)	1174-1235 (569-633)	Ush (Transoxania), Delhi	Mihrawli (near Delhi)
Ḥaḍrat Farīduddīn Mas'ūd Ganj-i Shakar (r.a.)	1175-1265 (570-664)	Multan, Hansi, Pakpatan (near Lahore)	Pakpatan
Ḥaḍrat Khwājah Niẓāmuddīn Awliyā' (r.a.)	1243/4-1325 (640/1-726)	Bada'un (east of Delhi)	Delhi
Ḥaḍrat Naṣīruddīn Chirāgh-i Delhī (r.a.)	1276/7-1356 (675-757)	Ayodhya (India), Delhi	Delhi
Ḥaḍrat Kamāluddīn 'Allāma (r.a.)			Gujurat (India)
Ḥaḍrat Sirājuddīn (r.a.)	d. 1411 (814)	Bengal, Delhi	Ahmadabad (India)
Ḥaḍrat 'Ilmuddīn (r.a.)			
Ḥaḍrat Maḥmūd (r.a.)			
Ḥaḍrat Jamāluddīn (r.a.)		Hansi (near Delhi)	
Ḥaḍrat Ḥasan (r.a.)			
Ḥaḍrat Muḥammad (r.a.)			
Ḥaḍrat Muḥammad Yaḥyā Madanī (r.a.)			
Ḥaḍrat Mawlānā Kalīmullāh Jahānābādī (r.a.)	d. 1729 (1142)		Delhi
Ḥaḍrat Mawlānā Niẓāmuddīn (r.a.)			Awrangabad (India)

Ḥaḍrat Mawlānā Fakhruddīn (r.a.)	d. 1784 (1199)		Delhi
Ḥaḍrat Mawlānā Shāh Niyāz Aḥmad (r.a.)	d. 1834 (1250)	Delhi	Bareilly
Ḥaḍrat Mawlānā Shaykh Miskīn (r.a.)			
Ḥaḍrat Mawlānā Nijabet 'Alī Shāh (r.a.)			
Ḥaḍrat Abū Ḥamid Karīm Bakhsh (r.a.)			
Ḥaḍrat Sayyid 'Abd al-Bārī Shāh (r.a.)	1859-1900 (1276-1318)	Balgadhi (Bengal), Calcutta	Bandel (West Bengal)
Ḥaḍrat Ḥāfiẓ Ḥāmid Ḥasan 'Alawī (r.a.)	1871/72-1959 (1288-1378)		Gonda (India)
Ḥaḍrat Muḥammad Sa'īd Khān (r.a.)	1907-1976 (1325-1396)		Azamgarh (India)
Ḥaḍrat Azad Rasool	b. 1921 (1339)	Rajistan (India)	

Qādirī	Dates	Place Born or Lived	Place Died
The Prophet Muḥammad ﷺ	570-632 (51 B.H. - 10 A.H.)	Mecca, Medina	Medina
The Caliph Ḥaḍrat 'Alī ibn Abī Ṭalib ؓ	c. 598-661 (c. 24 B.H. - 41 A.H.)	Mecca, Medina	Kufah
Ḥaḍrat Imām Ḥusayn ؓ	626-680 (4-60)	Medina	Karbala'
Ḥaḍrat Imām 'Alī Zayn al-'Ābidīn (r.a.)	d. 712 (93)		
Ḥaḍrat Imām Muḥammad Bāqir (r.a.)	d. 731 (113)		
Ḥaḍrat Imām Jā'far aṣ-Ṣādiq (r.a.)	702-765 (83-148)	Medina	Medina
Ḥaḍrat Imām Mūsā al-Kāẓim (r.a.)	d. 799 (183)		
Ḥaḍrat Imām Mūsā Riḍā (r.a.)	d. 818 (202)		
Ḥaḍrat Ma'rūf Karkhī (r.a.)	d. 815/16 (200)	Iran, Baghdad	Baghdad
Ḥaḍrat Sarī Saqaṭī (r.a.)	769-867/68 (152-253)	Baghdad	Baghdad
Ḥaḍrat Junayd Baghdādī (r.a.)	d. 910 (298)	Baghdad	Baghdad
Ḥaḍrat Shaykh Abū Bakr Shiblī (r.a.)	861-946 (247-334)	Baghdad, Samara	Baghdad
Ḥaḍrat Shaykh 'Abd al-'Azīz Tamīmī (r.a.)	d. 634 (425)		
Ḥaḍrat Abū al-Faḍl Abū al-Wāḥid Tamīmī (r.a.)			
Ḥaḍrat Abū al-Faraḥ Tarṭūsī (r.a.)			
Ḥaḍrat Abū al-Ḥasan Farshī (r.a.)	d. 1093 (486)		
Ḥaḍrat Abū Sa'īd al-Mubārak Mukharrimī (r.a.)	d. 1119 (513)		
Ḥaḍrat Shaykh 'Abd al-Qādir Jīlānī (r.a.)	1077/78-1116	Jilan (Persia) (470-561)	Baghdad
Ḥaḍrat Sayyid 'Abd al-Bārī Shāh (r.a.)	1859-1900 (1276-1318)	Balgadhi (Bengal), Calcutta	Bandel (West Bengal)
Ḥaḍrat Ḥāfiẓ Ḥāmid Ḥasan 'Alawī (r.a.)	1871/72-1959 (1288-1378)		Gonda (India)
Ḥaḍrat Muḥammad Sa'īd Khān (r.a.)	1907-1976 (1325-1396)		Azamgarh (India)
Ḥaḍrat Azad Rasool	b. 1921 (1339)	Rajistan (India)	